Test
Your English
Vocabulary
in Use

pre-intermediate & intermediate

Stuart Redman &
Ruth Gairns

CAMBRIDGE
UNIVERSITY PRESS

PUBLISHED BY THE PRESS SYNDICATE OF THE UNIVERSITY OF CAMBRIDGE
The Pitt Building, Trumpington Street, Cambridge, United Kingdom

CAMBRIDGE UNIVERSITY PRESS
The Edinburgh Building, Cambridge CB2 2RU, UK
40 West 20th Street, New York, NY 10011–4211, USA
477 Williamstown Road, Port Melbourne, VIC 3207, Australia
Ruiz de Alarcón 13, 28014 Madrid, Spain
Dock House, The Waterfront. Cape Town 8001, South Africa

http://www.cambridge.org

First published 2000
Reprinted 2002

Printed in the United Kingdom at the University Press, Cambridge

Typeface: Sabon   *System:* QuarkXPress 4 (Apple Macintosh)

A catalogue record for this book is available from the British Library

ISBN 0 521 77980 4 paperback

Contents

Connecting and linking

Topics

The world around us

People

Daily life

Work

Acknowledgements

We are very grateful to all the schools, institutions, teachers and students around the world who either piloted or commented on the material:

Olga Afanasyeva, Moscow, Russia
Brian Cracknell, Language Works, Singapore
Helen Donaghue, Edinburgh, UK
John Dowling, Paris, France
Erryl Griffiths, Cambridge, UK
Jan Krysiak and Tadeusz Wolanski, Gdańsk, Poland
Mary Lewandowska, Elbląg, Poland
Elena Marinina, Moscow, Russia
Geraldine Mark, Cheltenham, UK
Ewa Modrzejewska, Gdynia, Poland
Matthew Norbury, Edinburgh, UK
Chris Robinson, Stockport, UK
Sarah Schechter, Cambridge, UK
Davee Schulte, Seoul, South Korea
Chen Pei Tsen, Tainan County, Taiwan
Susan Tesar, Cambridge, UK
Louise Victor, Oxford, UK
Olga Vinogradova, Moscow, Russia

At Cambridge University Press, we would like to thank Nóirín Burke for setting up and supervising the project, and Jane Cordell for co-ordinating the piloting and for her excellent comments on the manuscript.

Finally, our thanks to Alyson Maskell for her highly professional and efficient editing of the material.

Introduction

Who is this book for?

Test your English Vocabulary in Use (pre-intermediate and intermediate) is designed to help students assess their vocabulary learning. It can be used independently as a testing book, or by learners who are using *English Vocabulary in Use (pre-intermediate and intermediate)* and want to assess their progress. Learners can use this test book on their own, but it can also be used by a teacher working with groups of students in a classroom.

For those who have not worked with *English Vocabulary in Use (pre-intermediate and intermediate)*, this book is recommended for learners at intermediate level.

How is the book organised?

Tests 1–3 corresponds to Units 1–3 in *English Vocabulary in Use (pre-intermediate and intermediate)*; the remaining tests all test vocabulary in the corresponding units of *English Vocabulary in Use (pre-intermediate and intermediate)*. The Contents page shows you how the tests are grouped by category. Every test is independent and you do not need to do the tests in a particular order, as they do not become progressively more difficult.

Each test has a total of 30 marks, and the number of marks for the exercises is given within each test. There is an Answer key at the back of the book.

Some words in the Answer key are also given in phonetic symbols, to help with pronunciation. A list of the phonetic symbols is given on page 142.

Also at the back of the book, you will find a Personal diary. Here, you can make a note of the words you found difficult to remember.

How to use this book

If you are working alone with this book, first look at the Contents page, and choose the tests that interest you. You will find different types of vocabulary test, such as tests on word formation, tests on different topic areas, tests on linking words. Try to do different kinds of test to give you variety. Remember, you do not need to do the tests in a particular order.

If you are using *English Vocabulary in Use (pre-intermediate and intermediate)*, you can use the tests after finishing a unit from the book. You can do this immediately after finishing a unit, or wait a while, e.g. a week, and use the test as a revision exercise.

You can use the tests more than once by writing the answers in pencil and rubbing them out when you have checked your answers. Alternatively, you could write your answers on a separate sheet of paper.

When you have checked your answers, you could write any words you had problems with in your Personal diary.

The marking scheme

You will find notes on the marking scheme at the beginning of the Answer key on page 104. The marking scheme is just to give you an idea of how well you know the vocabulary, but you do not have to use it.

1–3 Learning and recording vocabulary

This first page tests vocabulary from Units 1–3 of *English Vocabulary in Use*.

1–3.1
5 marks

Pictures are a good way to record and remember the meaning of certain words. Draw pictures of the following:

saucepan   knife   finger   thumb   smile

1–3.2
5 marks

You can increase your vocabulary by learning words and their opposites together. Complete the conversations with opposites of the underlined words. Look at the example.

Example: Did you like the film?

No, I ..**hated**.. it.

1 A: Did they <u>win</u> the match?
   B: No, they ....
2 A: Was the room <u>clean</u> when you arrived?
   B: No, it was very ....
3 A: Do they think inflation will <u>rise</u>?
   B: No, they say it is going to ....

4 A: Were all the staff <u>polite</u>?
   B: No, one of the waiters was very
   ....
5 A: Did you think the town was <u>beautiful</u>?
   B: No, I thought it was really
   ....

1–3.3
4 marks

Match each verb on the left with two of the nouns on the right.

1 put on
2 take
3 do
4 make

a mistake   homework
weight   half an hour
a photo   your gloves
an exercise   a mess

1–3.4
5 marks

Circle the correct <u>underlined</u> word or phrase.

1 If you do something silently, it means you do it <u>noisily / without a noise</u>.
2 If the price of something rises sharply, it means it rises <u>a lot / a little</u>.
3 If you revise something, it means you <u>study it / study it again</u>.
4 If something (e.g. a time or place) suits you, it means that time or place <u>is / isn't</u> convenient for you and acceptable to you.
5 If you are homesick, it means you are <u>ill / unhappy because you are away from home</u>.

1–3.5
5 marks

Complete this table.

Verb	Noun
explain	....
....	choice
define	....
translate	....
....	pronunciation

1–3.6
6 marks

The pronunciation of new words can be difficult. Is the pronunciation of the <u>underlined</u> letters in each pair of words the same or different?

Your score
/30

1 h<u>o</u>mework / l<u>o</u>se
2 l<u>ou</u>d / d<u>ou</u>bt
3 s<u>i</u>lent / <u>i</u>sland

4 <u>a</u>che / <u>ch</u>oose
5 w<u>eigh</u>t / rec<u>ei</u>pt
6 dr<u>ea</u>m / l<u>ea</u>st

English language words

4.1

12 marks

Read the text and identify each <u>underlined</u> part of speech (noun, verb, adjective, etc.). Write your answers in the space below. The first one has been done for you.

We ⁽⁰⁾<u>walked</u> along the main ⁽¹⁾<u>street</u> between the workers' cottages and ⁽²⁾<u>the</u> only hotel in the town. A few people ⁽³⁾<u>passed</u> by – two women ⁽⁴⁾<u>in</u> smart suits, a very ⁽⁵⁾<u>large</u> man walking a small dog, and ⁽⁶⁾<u>a</u> boy pushing his ⁽⁷⁾<u>bicycle</u> while singing ⁽⁸⁾<u>quietly</u> to himself. The weather was still ⁽⁹⁾<u>miserable</u> and ⁽¹⁰⁾<u>we</u> could feel a few drops ⁽¹¹⁾<u>of</u> rain falling as we ⁽¹²⁾<u>turned</u> the corner and saw the station in the distance.

Example: ...verb...

1 ....
2 ....
3 ....

4 ....
5 ....
6 ....

7 ....
8 ....
9 ....

10 ....
11 ....
12 ....

4.2

6 marks

Answer these questions.

1 Is *information* an uncountable noun or a plural noun?
2 Is *trousers* uncountable or plural?
3 Is *news* uncountable or plural?
4 What kind of verb are *get off*, *put sth. on* and *look sth. up*?
5 What do we call the base form of a verb such as *say*, *tell* or *start*?
6 What do we call a group of words (a phrase or even a sentence) with a particular meaning that is different from any of the individual words?

4.3

7 marks

Complete these sentences with the correct word.

1 In the word *unfriendly*, **un-** is called a ....
2 In the word *comfortable*, **-able** is called a ....
3 *Fantastic* is a .... of *marvellous*.
4 *Large* is the .... of *small*.
5 /dɪ'saɪd/ and /fæn'tæstɪk/ show words written in .... symbols.
6 The word *decide* has two .... and *fantastic* has three ....
7 On the words *de<u>ci</u>de* and *fan<u>ta</u>stic*, the main .... is underlined.

4.4

5 marks

What do we call the punctuation marks that are circled in these sentences?

Example: ⓈShe sat down quietly. ...*capital letter*...

1 They arrived on time⊙ ....

2 What are you doing⊘ ....

3 I lost my ticket⊙ so I had to buy another one. ....

4 Most of the students⊙15 altogether⊙came to the concert. ....

5 They were all very well⊙dressed. ....

5 Problems with pronunciation

5.1
8 marks
Match the words in each group that contain the same <u>underlined</u> vowel sound. The first one has been done for you.

Group 1
thr<u>ou</u>gh   h<u>o</u>t
en<u>ou</u>gh   sp<u>oo</u>n
c<u>ou</u>gh   tr<u>ou</u>ble

Group 2
d<u>i</u>et   mach<u>i</u>ne
s<u>i</u>nce   <u>i</u>sland
pol<u>i</u>ce   oppos<u>i</u>te

Group 3
<u>a</u>ccent   f<u>a</u>st
pot<u>a</u>to   p<u>a</u>lace
c<u>a</u>lm   r<u>a</u>zor

5.2
6 marks
In each line, underline the word which is stressed differently from the other three words.

Example: remember   decided   expensive   <u>industry</u>

1 symptom   sunbathe   palace   prefer
2 interested   understand   opposite   policy
3 cathedral   assistance   organise   remember
4 hyphen   police   decide   machine
5 accent   virus   machine   desert
6 advertisement   competition   psychology   grammatical

5.3
9 marks
Choose the correct pronunciation and answer questions 1–9 using the phonetic symbols.

KNIFE /naɪf/ or /knaɪf/   AISLE /aɪl/ or /aɪsl/   HANDSOME /ˈhændsəm/ or /ˈhænsəm/
FASTEN /ˈfaːstən/ or /ˈfaːsən/   WRIST /wrɪst/ or /rɪst/   KNEE /kniː/ or /niː/
BOMB /bɒmb/ or /bɒm/   HONEST /ˈhɒnɪst/ or /ˈɒnɪst/   LISTEN /ˈlɪstən/ or /ˈlɪsən/
CHRISTMAS /ˈkrɪsməs/ or /ˈkrɪstməs/

Example: You do this to music or the radio. ...../ˈlɪsən/.....

1 This is between your hand and your arm. ....
2 This is where you walk on a plane to get to your seat. ....
3 If you are this, you tell the truth. ....
4 The joint in the middle of your leg. ....
5 If this explodes, it can be very dangerous. ....
6 You can describe an attractive-looking man as this. ....
7 You do this to your seat belt in a car or on a plane. ....
8 You need this for cutting your food. ....
9 A religious festival celebrated towards the end of December. ....

5.4
7 marks
All the pictures are of words which contain the /ə/ sound at least once. Label the drawings and circle the (/ə/). Look at the example first.

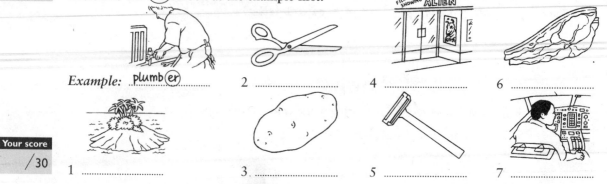

Example: plumb(er)

2 ....
4 ....
6 ....

1 ....
3 ....
5 ....
7 ....

Your score
/30

Test your English Vocabulary in Use (pre-intermediate and intermediate)

Classroom language

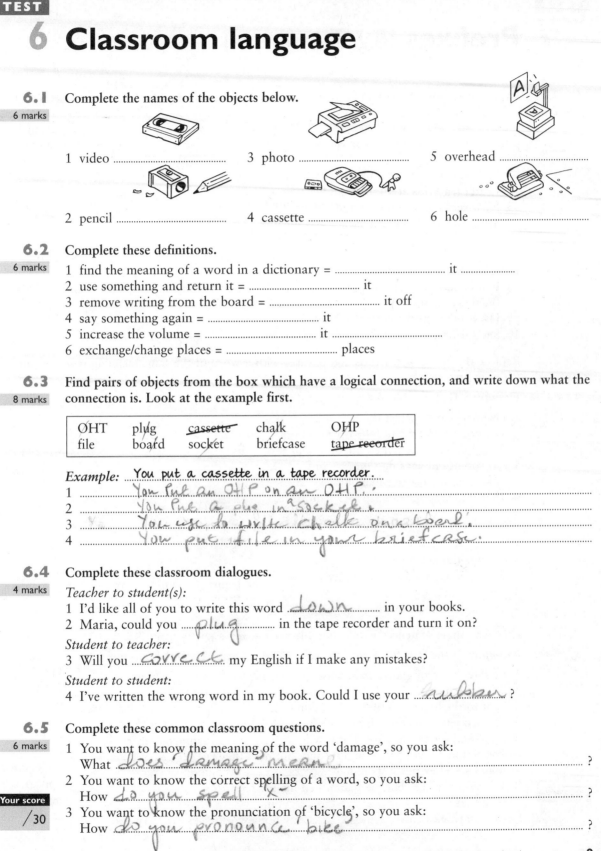

6.1 Complete the names of the objects below.

6 marks

1 video .... 3 photo .... 5 overhead ....

2 pencil .... 4 cassette .... 6 hole ....

6.2 Complete these definitions.

6 marks

1 find the meaning of a word in a dictionary = ... it ....

2 use something and return it = ... it

3 remove writing from the board = ... it off

4 say something again = ... it

5 increase the volume = ... it ....

6 exchange/change places = ... places

6.3 Find pairs of objects from the box which have a logical connection, and write down what the

8 marks connection is. Look at the example first.

OHT	plug	~~cassette~~	chalk	OHP
file	board	socket	briefcase	~~tape recorder~~

Example: You put a cassette in a tape recorder.

1 .... You put an OHP on an OHP.

2 .... You put a plug in socket.

3 .... You use to write chalk on a board.

4 .... You put file in your briefcase.

6.4 Complete these classroom dialogues.

4 marks

Teacher to student(s):

1 I'd like all of you to write this word ....down........ in your books.

2 Maria, could you ....plug........ in the tape recorder and turn it on?

Student to teacher:

3 Will you ....correct........ my English if I make any mistakes?

Student to student:

4 I've written the wrong word in my book. Could I use your ....rubber........ ?

6.5 Complete these common classroom questions.

6 marks

1 You want to know the meaning of the word 'damage', so you ask:
What ....does 'damage' mean.. ?

2 You want to know the correct spelling of a word, so you ask:
How ....do you spell x~.. ?

3 You want to know the pronunciation of 'bicycle', so you ask:
How ....do you pronounce 'bike'.. ?

7 Prefixes (e.g. *un-, dis-, re-*)

7.1

10 marks

Use a prefix from the left and a word from the right and complete the sentences below.

un-	in-	ir-
im-	il-	dis-

possible	friendly	regular	legible	patient
correct	honest	visible	employed	responsible

1 Nobody at the party talked to us – they were very ....
2 I can't read this at all; her handwriting is completely *illegible* ....
3 It's a very depressed area and almost 20% of young adults are ....
4 You can't see where my jacket was mended. The repair is completely *invisible* .. .
5 I find it very hard to remember the past tense of lots of .... verbs.
6 Bob's so *impatient* .... that he's just not prepared to wait for the right opportunity.
7 It was very *incorrect* .... to go out and leave those two children alone.
8 It says here we lost £300 last week, but these figures must be .... Check them again, Sue!
9 His brother steals money and tells lies – he's very ....
10 She says it can't be done, but I don't accept that. Nothing is ....

7.2

6 marks

Replace the <u>underlined</u> words and phrases with a word of the same meaning which begins with the prefix given.

Example: That child looks very <u>sad</u>. un.**happy** ....

1 I'm sure that's <u>against the law</u>. il.*legal* ....
2 The doctor told me to <u>take off my clothes</u>. un.*dress* ....
3 We <u>don't have the same opinion</u> about this. dis.*agreement* ....
4 His room is always <u>in a mess</u>. un.*tidy* ....
5 I'm afraid she <u>doesn't like</u> onions. dis.*like* ....
6 That was very <u>rude</u>, wasn't it? im.*polite* ....

7.3

5 marks

Match the prefixes in the box with the meanings below. (There are *two* prefixes for one meaning.)

1 do something again
2 do something badly or incorrectly
3 reverse an action
4 do something too much

mis-	un-	over-	re-	dis-

7.4

9 marks

Complete these sentences with a suitable verb, using a prefix from 7.3.

Example: If she fails her exam, she can ...**retake**........... it in the autumn.

1 I wrote the wrong answer because I *misunderstood* the question.
2 When I *oversleep* .... I feel even more tired when I wake up.
3 I got to the hotel at 4.00 but I couldn't *unpack* ..... my stuff until later.
4 I turned left instead of right. Obviously I *misheard* ...... what she said.
5 It's closed for the summer, but it will *reopen* .... in September.
6 The children were here a minute ago, but now they've *disappeared*
7 John had a key but it wouldn't *unlock* .... the door.
8 A: It says here £3, but the man asked me for £5.
   B: In that case he has *overcharged* you.
9 Do you think I can *redo* .... my homework if it's not very good?

| take |
| pack |
| do |
| open |
| lock |
| sleep |
| understand |
| appear |
| hear |
| charge |

8 Noun suffixes (e.g. *-ion, -ity, -ment*)

8.1 Complete the sentences with the correct form of the word on the right.

10 marks

Example: Who made the __arrangements__ for the meeting?　　ARRANGE

1　We had a very heated __discussion__ in class today.　　DISCUSS
2　I think __punctuality__ is very important.　　PUNCTUAL
3　The __organisation__ of the festival was excellent.　　ORGANISE
4　Who won the __election__?　　ELECT
5　He's never been very good at __spelling__.　　SPELL
6　Their __happiness__ is all that matters to me.　　HAPPY
7　The __similarity__ between them is incredible.　　SIMILAR
8　Has there been much __improvement__ lately?　　IMPROVE
9　Have they got all the __information__ they need?　　INFORM
10　This animal only appears during the hours of __darkness__.　　DARK

8.2 Complete the crossword. What is the **opposite** of the word in the tinted box?

8 marks

1　the opposite of 'clever'

2　running for pleasure and to keep fit

3　to 'get better'

4　to talk about something in a serious way

5　to choose someone by voting for them

6　someone who arrives at the right time is this

7　someone who paints pictures

1 STUPID
2 JOGGING
3 IMPROVE
4 DISCUSS
5 ELECT
6 PUNCTUAL
7 ARTIST

The opposite of the word in the box is ....

8.3 Complete these tables and **underline** the main stress as in the example.

6 marks

Verb	General noun	Adjective	Noun
educate	education	popular	popularity
manage	management	weak	weakness
translate	translation	stupid	stupidity
hesitate	hesitate		

8.4 What do we call these people?

6 marks

Example: a person who *dances* __dancer__

1　a person who murders someone
2　a person who acts
3　a person who works in economics
4　a person who farms
5　a person who translates
6　a person who employs other people
7　a person who works in psychology
8　a person who sings
9　a person who operates something
10　a person who plays football
11　a person who directs films
12　a person who writes articles in a newspaper

9 Adjective suffixes (e.g. -able, -ful, -y)

9.1 Add the correct suffix: -able or -ible.

9 marks

1 The food was ined*ible*.
2 The coffee was undrink*able*.
3 My bed is very comfort*able*.
4 Her shoes were very unsuit*able*.
5 The film was very enjoy*able*.
6 My working hours are very flex*able*.
7 The buses are usually reli*able*.
8 The doctor's writing was incomprehens*able*.
9 These cups are unbreak*able*.

9.2 Complete the following dialogues with adjectives ending in -less.

5 marks

1 A: Did you find the book useful?
   B: No, it was completely *useless* .
2 A: Did the injection hurt?
   B: No, fortunately it was *painless* .
3 A: Has he got somewhere to live?
   B: No, the poor man is *homeless* .
4 A: That was a very silly mistake, wasn't it?
   B: Yes, it was *careless* of me – I wasn't concentrating.
5 A: Dorothy never thinks about other people; she didn't even phone to say she wasn't
      coming tonight.
   B: Yes, I agree – she's really quite *thoughtless* .

9.3 Circle the correct word.

7 marks

1 He can play ten ~~musical~~/music instruments.
2 It is an ~~economic~~/economical car to run: it can do 20 kilometres on a litre of petrol.
3 I'm not sure if this sweater is washing/~~washable~~ or not.
4 My sister is very ~~knowledgeable~~/knowledge about gardening, but I'm afraid I don't know
   the first thing about it.
5 He's a member of one of the extreme politic/~~political~~ parties, but I can't remember which.
6 People say that you have to be very created/~~creative~~ to be successful in advertising.
7 I didn't think it was a very attracted/~~attractive~~ place.

9.4 Rewrite the sentences using an adjective formed from the words in *italics*. The meaning must
stay the same.

5 marks

Example: When the *sun* comes out, I always feel better.
        When it *is sunny, I always feel better.*

1 There is too much *cloud* to see the stars tonight.
   It *is too cloudy to see the stars tonight.*
2 If there is still *fog* in an hour, we will have to cancel the trip.
   If it's *still foggy in an hour we'll have to cancel.*
3 There's a lot of *industry* in the town.
   It's a very *industrial in the town*
4 There is a lot of *dirt* in that corner of the room.
   That corner of the room *is dirty*
5 She knows about the *dangers* of drugs.
   She knows that *drugs are dangerous*

9.5 Which four nouns below form adjectives with the suffix -ful?

4 marks

pain   help   home   thought   fame   care

Test your English Vocabulary in Use (pre-intermediate and intermediate)

Nouns, verbs and adjectives with the same form (*to dream, a dream*)

10.1
8 marks

Label the pictures with verbs from the box.

| laugh | pull | taste | smile | dream | clean | queue | ache |

1 ~~smile~~   3 ~~pull~~   5 ~~ach~~   7 ~~laugh~~

2 ~~dream~~   4 ~~queue~~   6 ~~clean~~   8 ~~taste~~

1 mark   Seven of these verbs can also be used as nouns with no change in form, and one can be used as an adjective with no change in form. Which one?

10.2
6 marks

Match the verbs on the left with the nouns on the right.

1 answer   4 guess
2 damage   5 smell
3 dry   6 push

a the dishes   d the perfume
b the phone   e the answer
c the button   f the side of the car

1 mark   Which of these verbs can also be used as an adjective?

10.3
14 marks

Rewrite the sentences below. Use the underlined verbs as nouns and include a verb from the box. Make any changes that are necessary. Look at the examples first.

| have (×3) | give (×2) | wait | go on | send | put on |

Examples: Let's walk for a bit, then <u>rest</u>.   Let's walk for a bit, then have a rest.

Don't <u>brake</u> too suddenly.   Don't put on the brakes too suddenly.

1 Did you <u>reply</u> to the invitation? *Did send reply to the invitation.*
2 Could you <u>look</u> at this report for me? *Could you in look at this report for me.*
3 People <u>diet</u> for all sorts of reasons. *People go on diet all sorts of reasons.*
4 If you don't know the answer, just <u>guess</u>. *If you dont know the answer, ...*
5 Someone <u>pushed</u> me and I fell over. *Some gave me pushed*
6 We had to <u>queue</u> for ages. *We had to wait queue*
7 Why don't you <u>ring</u> her when she gets back? *Why dont you give ring*

11 Compound nouns (e.g. *living room, coffee cup*)

11.1
8 marks

Complete these definitions with the correct compound noun.

1 Your first language is also called your *mother* tongue .
2 Stories about the future are called *science* fiction .
3 The place where you buy tickets for the theatre or cinema is the *box* office .
4 Someone who looks after children when the parents are out is a *baby-* sitter .
5 A long line of cars moving slowly is a *traffic* jam .
6 The room where you eat meals is the .... *room.*
7 Tax you pay on your salary is called .... *tax.*
8 Your sister's husband or your husband's brother is your .... *-in-* ....

11.2
8 marks

Label these pictures with the correct compound noun.

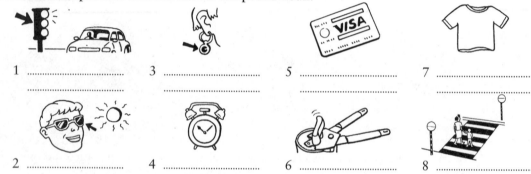

1 .... 3 .... 5 .... 7 ....

2 .... 4 .... 6 .... 8 ....

11.3
4 marks

Add two more words in each group to form compound nouns.

1 traffic lights
  traffic ....
  traffic ....

2 box office
  .... office
  .... office

3 bedroom
  .... room
  .... room

4 brother-in-law
  .... -in-law
  .... -in-law

11.4
6 marks

Match a word from the left with a word from the right to form six compound nouns.

1 first   a meter   ....
2 cheque   b machine   ....
3 film   c book   ....
4 washing   d paper   ....
5 parking   e aid   ....
6 writing   f star   ....

11.5
4 marks

Complete these sentences with a suitable compound noun.

1 Famous rock star include Elton John, Michael Jackson and Madonna.
2 I brought my toothbrush, but I forgot the toothpaste, so I just had to use water.
3 And my hair was wet for ages because I forgot to bring my hairdryer.
4 I think the Chinese word is 'ping pong', but we call it table tennis .

Your score

/30

12.1 Complete the compound adjectives in these dialogues.

8 marks

1 A: Look at him. He's famous, isn't he?
   B: Yes, he's very well-*know* .

2 A: What a handsome man!
   B: Yes, he is good-*looking* , isn't he?

3 A: Do nurses earn a good salary?
   B: No, they are badly-*paid* .

4 A: Julie's so relaxed, isn't she?
   B: Yes, I find her very easy-*going* too.

5 A: They've got plenty of money.
   B: Yes, they're not badly-*off* .

6 A: So you work all day?
   B: Yes. It's a full-*time* job.

7 A: That lady always looks so smart.
   B: Yes, she's very well-*dress* .

8 A: Those children are always so good.
   B: Yes, they're very well-*behaver*

12.2 Re-order these words to form sentences. Add a hyphen (-) where necessary.

5 marks

1 bill / I / yesterday / the / dollar / found / a / fifty / street / in
2 ten / to / it / a / drive / is / minute / only / office / my
3 delay / had / airport / hour / three / the / unfortunately / we / a / at
4 hotels / in / stay / star / movie / often / five / stars
5 a / child / can't / year / understand / you / old / expect / three / to

12.3 Complete the letter below with suitable compound adjectives from the box.

10 marks

| badly-paid | well-behaved | part-time | five-minute | four-month-old |
| easy-going | south-west | brand-new | six-year-old | well-off |

Dear Martha,

Well, I've arrived in London and I've been incredibly lucky – I found a job the day after I arrived here! I'm staying with an English family and I'm looking after the children. It's only a ⁽¹⁾ *part-time* job, so I'll be free in the mornings and evenings. The family are really nice – very relaxed and ⁽²⁾ *easy going* and the house is big and beautiful, so they are obviously quite ⁽³⁾ *brand new* . What's more, they've got a ⁽⁴⁾ *brand new* car which I'm allowed to drive when I'm collecting the children from school. There's a ⁽⁵⁾ *four month old* baby and ⁽⁶⁾ *six-year-old* twins who are very ⁽⁷⁾ *well-behaved* children, which makes life easy for me! The house is in ⁽⁸⁾ *south-west* London, which is a very pleasant area and it's near Wimbledon – only a ⁽⁹⁾ *five-minute* walk from the famous tennis club! The only problem is that looking after children is a ⁽¹⁰⁾ *badly-paid* job, but I <u>have</u> got free accommodation. Why don't you come and see me?

Love, Erica

12.4 Fill the gaps with a suitable word.

7 marks

1 I bought a second-*hand* coat but unfortunately it's very *badly*-made.
2 The film was well-*acted* (Tom Cruise was brilliant), but very *badly*-directed.
3 *left*-handed people find it more difficult to use normal scissors.

/30

4 He went out in the cold wearing only a short-*sleeved* shirt.
5 He managed to find a seat in the first-*class* section of the plane.

13 Collocation (word partners)

13.1 Correct the mistake in each of these sentences.

8 marks

1 He lost the bus and had to wait for the next one.
2 I do a lot of mistakes when I'm trying to speak German.
3 Her mother was very angry because she said a lie.
4 Unfortunately, I lost the lesson last week because I was sick.
5 My brother has wide shoulders, so buy him a large size.
6 Don't get on the car until I've taken all the shopping out.
7 My father says very funny jokes.
8 I had a big illness last summer and was in bed for two months.

13.2 Complete this speech, by the director of a chain of sports shops, using words from the box.

7 marks

range	success	important	aware	unlikely	majority	work

It has been a very difficult year for the company, as I am sure you are all fully
(1) ....aware........ . However, the good news is that it is now highly
(2) ....unlikely....... that we will have to close any of our shops or lose any
workers. This is thanks to all your hard (3) ....work......... , and I have to
congratulate especially those of you who work in the London branches of our
stores who have had great (4) ....success..... in selling a wide
(5) ....range...... of new ski clothes. The vast (6) ....majority....
of our customers are happy with the service we give them, and it is vitally
(7) ....important.... for us to continue to maintain these high standards in
the future. Thank you, everyone.

13.3 Are these sentences true? If not, change them to make them true.

8 marks

1 The opposite of a dry wine is a wet wine.
2 The opposite of dry weather is wet weather.
3 The opposite of a soft voice is a loud voice.
4 The opposite of a soft drink is a loud drink.
5 The opposite of strong coffee is weak coffee.
6 The opposite of a strong accent is a weak accent.
7 The opposite of a light smoker is strong smoker.
8 The opposite of light rain is heavy rain.

13.4 Cross out any incorrect collocations. Be careful: in some groups, they are all correct.

7 marks

1 to start a car
   to start a family
   to start a bicycle

2 a heavy smoker
   a heavy lesson
   heavy traffic

3 to get into/out of a car
   to get into/out of a taxi
   to get into/out of a bike

4 to tell a story
   to tell a lie
   to tell the truth

5 to get on/off a taxi
   to get on/off a bus
   to get on/off a plane

6 to miss a person
   to miss a train
   to miss a lesson

7 to run a kilometre
   to run a joke
   to run a business

Your score

/30

14 Verb or adjective + preposition

14.1
10 marks

Correct the mistake in each sentence.

1 I like listening the radio when I'm in the car. *on*
2 We might go out tomorrow, but it depends of the weather.
3 Venice is very different the rest of Italy.
4 He shouted to me because he was very angry.
5 Are you interested on sport?
6 She seems to be suffering by shock. *for*
7 I think she's going to apply that job at the post office.
8 I'm not very good in maths, so you'll have to add this up for me.
9 She's sitting by the phone, waiting a call.
10 He's always spending money for things he doesn't need.

14.2
8 marks

Complete these dialogues with a suitable preposition.

1 A: Was he angry?
  B: Yes, in fact he threw the book ....*at*.... me.
2 A: Did the engineer repair the fault?
  B: No, he didn't, so I had to complain ...*to*.... his boss.
3 A: Her boss is always criticising her.
  B: Yes, I know, and she's getting really tired ......*for*..... it.
4 A: Were you surprised ...*at/by*....his answer?
  B: No, not really.
5 A: Why is the phone making that strange noise?
  B: I don't know. There must be something wrong ....*with*....... it.
6 A: Can we get in?
  B: No, the room is full ....*of*..... boxes.
7 A: Did the girl in the flat upstairs phone you?
  B: She didn't need to – she just opened the window and shouted down ....*to*...... us.
8 A: My cousin's getting married ......*to*..... a friend of mine next week.
  B: Oh, so you'll be going to the wedding, then.

14.3
12 marks

Rewrite the sentences using the word on the right and the correct preposition. Start with the words you are given. The meaning must stay the same.

Example: He doesn't like spiders: they frighten him.
  He *is afraid of spiders.*   AFRAID

1 She said she was sorry about the mistake.
  She ....*apologised for the mistake*.... APOLOGISE
2 I think you are right.
  I ....*agree with*....   AGREE
3 This is my car.
  This car ....*belongs to me*....   BELONG
4 He knows about the problem.
  He ...*is aware of the problem.*....   AWARE
5 This book is like the other one.
  This book ...*is same the other one.*...   SIMILAR
6 I don't enjoy football very much.
  I am ....*very keen on football*....   KEEN

Your score
/30

15 Preposition + noun

15.1 Choose the correct preposition to complete these sentences.

12 marks

1 I think it was written ..by.... Charles Dickens.
2 We saw a film of it ..on...... TV.
3 Did you read that article ....in.... the paper?
4 He might take the train, but he'll probably come ...by....... coach.
5 I'm afraid Petra is ....with.... the phone – do you want to come in and wait?
6 ...In.... the morning, I always go ...for..... a run before breakfast if I've got time.
7 She says she did her homework ...by...... herself.
8 Bob Dylan wrote the first one, but the other songs were written ...by..... the band themselves.
9 I read something about Tarantino's new film ....in.... that magazine.
10 There's no noise here ...at.... night.
11 Shall we go out ....for.... a walk?

15.2 Choose a preposition from the left-hand box and a noun from the right-hand box to complete the sentences below.

8 marks

| on   by | mistake   strike   hand   purpose   foot |
| | chance   accident holiday   my own |

Example: These chocolates are all made .by.. hand..

1 I think they're away ..on.... holiday..
2 I'm sure he broke it ..by.... accident because he's a very nice person and would never do anything like that ...on.... purpose.
3 There has been a lot of trouble at the factory and about fifty of the workers have decided to go ....on.... strike.... from tomorrow.
4 I took it ..by..... mistake because it looks exactly like mine.
5 We met them ..by..... chance – it was an extraordinary coincidence.
6 I'd prefer to do it ....on.... my own...., because other people make me nervous.
7 If they aren't in a hurry, I think they'll come ...on.... foot...... .

15.3 Complete these definitions with the correct prepositional phrase.

4 marks

1 If you arrive at the exact time for an appointment, you arrive .on.. time....... .
2 And if you arrive for an appointment before the time you need to be there, then you arrive ...in.. time..... .
3 If you see a minimum of 20 clients every day, you see .... 20.
4 If you are unemployed and haven't got a job then you are ....

15.4 Circle the correct preposition in these sentences.

6 marks

1 I often go abroad in business / on business.
2 It took a long time but in the end / at the end we got there.
3 I'm going to speak to them at the moment / in a moment.
4 Who knows if it's true, but that's what I heard on the radio / in the radio.
5 We had a vote in the end / at the end of the meeting.
6 We've been in business / on business now for fifteen years.

16.1 With many phrasal verbs, the particle emphasises the meaning of the verb or gives the idea of
12 marks completing the action. Complete these phrasal verbs.

  1 I *woke* ...*up*... at 7.30, but I then went back to sleep.
  2 I'd better *hurry* ...*up*... and *send* ...*off*... that letter of application.
  3 Is she still *saving* ...*up*... for that CD player?
  4 I'll never *find* ...*out*... the name of that hotel we stayed in.
  5 I'm not feeling very well. I think I'd better *lie* ...*down*... on the bed.
  6 Shall we *eat* ...*up*... this rice we didn't finish last night?
  7 She *fell* ...*over*... and hurt her leg but I don't know exactly how it happened.
  8 Come on, *drink* ...*up*... , and then we can see the rest of the exhibition.
  9 We can *finish* ...*off*... this exercise tomorrow.
  10 I've been *standing* ...*up*... all day; I really must *sit* ...*down*... for ten minutes.

16.2 Choose the correct phrasal verb to complete each sentence.
5 marks

  1 I promised to ...*Look after*... her daughter next week when she's at work.
    a) take off   b) look for   c) look after   d) take after
  2 It took them ages to ...*put*... ...*out*... the fire.
    a) put off   b) take off   c) put out   d) put away
  3 It was quite a serious illness, so she took a while to ...*get*... ...*over*... it.
    a) get over   b) go over   c) take over   d) get through
  4 Don't leave that meat there too long – it'll ...*go*... ...*off*... .
    a) take off   b) go over   c) pass away   d) go off
  5 With inflation at 10%, the price could ...*go*... ...*up*... again quite soon.
    a) rise up   b) get up   c) go up   d) put up

16.3 Complete these sentences using a suitable phrasal verb.
8 marks

  1 I don't know this word. I'll have to .... it .... in the dictionary.
  2 A: Do you want us to stop now?
    B: No, you can .... for another ten minutes if you like.
  3 I used to smoke, but I .... it .... last year.
  4 A: Can we leave this rubbish here?
    B: No, I think we should .... it .... and put it in the bin over there.
  5 A: When will you finish typing those letters?
    B: Oh, I should .... most of them by the end of the morning.
  6 Hurry up! Your plane .... in about 40 minutes.
  7 A: Do you have a good relationship with your parents?
    B: Not when I was younger, but I .... very well .... them now.
  8 A: Shall we have another sandwich?
    B: We can't, I'm afraid. I've .... bread.

16.4 Replace the <u>underlined</u> words with a phrasal verb with the same meaning.
5 marks

  1 What time shall I <u>collect</u> your suit from the dry cleaner's?
  2 There was a warning at three o'clock and then the bomb <u>exploded</u> five minutes later.
  3 I was so nervous I didn't think I would <u>pass</u> the exam.
  4 Do you mind if I <u>remove</u> my jacket and tie?
  5 The alarm didn't <u>ring</u> this morning – there must be something wrong with it.

17 Phrasal verbs 2

These exercises also test some of the phrasal verbs from Test 16.

17.1 **Correct any mistakes in these sentences. Be careful: some are correct.**

8 marks

1 She got the train off and went into the coffee bar. ─┤
2 Take your shoes off.
3 A: Mum, where are my shoes?
   B: Here they are. Put on them quickly!
4 I've decided to stay this weekend in. ✗
5 The children are growing quickly up. ✓
6 Lie down over there.
7 Could you turn the TV on, please?
8 I woke at 7 o'clock up. ─┤

17.2 **Describe each picture with a sentence containing a phrasal verb.**

12 marks

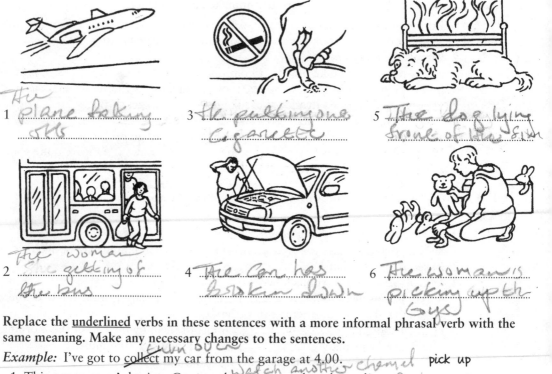

1 The plane taking off
2 The woman she getting off the bus
3 He putting one cigarette
4 The car has broken down
5 The dog lying front of the fire
6 The woman is picking up the toys

17.3 **Replace the underlined verbs in these sentences with a more informal phrasal verb with the same meaning. Make any necessary changes to the sentences.**

10 marks

Example: I've got to <u>collect</u> my car from the garage at 4.00.   turn over   **pick up**

1 This programme's boring. Can we <u>change to another channel</u>?   watch another channel / find one
2 I heard she lost her job, but I couldn't <u>discover</u> any more details.   turn off
3 Could you <u>increase the volume on</u> the television? I can't hear it.
4 It doesn't have to be a true story – you can <u>invent</u> it.   make up
5 Thieves <u>entered</u> the art gallery <u>illegally</u> and stole a Picasso.   broke into
6 We're late because the car <u>stopped working</u> on the way.
7 He opened the door and <u>entered</u>.   come/was walking   come up   leave / miss out
8 The price of meat has <u>increased</u> a lot this year.
9 Do that page of exercises again, but this time, <u>omit</u> the middle one.
10 I just can't <u>manage</u> in London on £80 a week.   get by

18 Idioms and fixed expressions

18.1
8 marks

Match the <u>underlined</u> expressions on the left with a word or expression on the right.

1 <u>Hang on</u> a minute!   a decide
2 I can <u>make do</u> with £10.   b want
3 <u>Never mind</u>, I'll do it later.   c come
4 I'm a bit <u>tied up</u> at the moment.   d manage
5 <u>Go ahead</u> – I don't need it.   e wait
6 I can't <u>make it</u> to your party, I'm afraid.   f help yourself
7 Do you <u>feel like</u> a coffee?   g busy
8 Come on – <u>make up your mind</u>!   h it doesn't matter

18.2
12 marks

Choose a verb from the box on the left and a noun from the box on the right to complete the idiom in the sentences below. Put the verb in the correct tense.

give	make	pull	keep		leg	mind	ring	move
get	make	take			eye	matters	turns	

Example: I can't speak to him now – please tell him I'll ....give.... him a ..ring.. .

1 Don't believe anything he tells you – he's just ...pulling... your ..legs.......... .
2 He wants me to ...keep......... an ..eye...... on the children while he is out.
3 Come on – ...make...... a ...move..... on. You're going to be late.
4 It was cold and raining, and to ...make.... ..matters.... worse, we were already an hour late.
5 A: Do I have to decide right now?
   B: No, but you'll have to ...make..... up your ...mind...... by tomorrow.
6 I don't always cook supper. My husband and I ...take..... it in ...turns....... .

18.3
5 marks

Complete the idioms in the dialogues. Notice that B always agrees with A.

1 A: She really likes him, doesn't she?
   B: Yes, she *is* ...mad.......... *about* him.
2 A: They enjoyed themselves at the party, didn't they?
   B: Yes, they *had a good* ...time...... .
3 A: Did they go the quick way?
   B: Yes, they *took a short* ...cut...... .
4 A: They'll never come back here again, will they?
   B: No, they have gone *for* ...good........ .
5 A: Do they annoy each other?
   B: Yes, they *get on each other's* ...cut............ .

18.4
5 marks

Circle the correct word.

1 I've never been very good at little/(small) talk.
2 I couldn't tell you the answer (offhand)/offhands – I'll have to look it up.
3 The changes will be good for us in the (long)/large term.
4 I don't think they'll come to the exhibition; (in)/for a start, they aren't really interested in art.
5 A: What's (up)/off?
   B: Nothing – why do you ask?

Your score /30

19 Make, do, have, take

19.1 Fill the gaps with the correct verb (*make*, *do*, *have* or *take*).

8 marks

1 It's a nice restaurant. I ...*had*... baked fish in a spicy tomato sauce and it was really good.
2 If he's going to be a dentist, he should ...*make*... lots of money.
3 Why did you decide to ...*take*... a taxi from the airport? The underground is much quicker and cheaper.
4 We've decided that we're going to ...*have*... a party at the end of the course.
5 It's incredibly hot. I think I'm going to ...*have*... a cold shower.
6 We don't have much food in the house, so I suppose I'll have to go out and ...*do*... some shopping.
7 It's been a busy week, so I'm going to ...*have*... a rest this weekend.
8 A: Did you ...*do*... anything last night?
  B: No, I stayed at home.

19.2 Complete these sentences with *make* or *do* and a suitable noun.

14 marks

1 The flat is dirty because I never ...*do*... any *cleaning*.
2 My English is terrible. I ...*make*... *mistakes* every time I open my mouth and try to speak.
3 A: How many ...*subjects*... do you ...*do*... at school?
  B: About twelve including two languages and all the sciences.
4 I ...*did*... two ...*exams*... yesterday but I don't think I've passed either of them.
5 It was impossible to work because there was a party in the flat below. They had a disco and they were ...*made*... so much ...*noise*... .
6 A: Is she still at university?
  B: Yes. She's studying for her Master's degree, and she's ...*doing*... *research* in the field of microbiology.
7 I didn't do very well in my course at first, but I've improved a lot and my teacher says I'm ...*making*... really good ...*progress*... now.

19.3 Cross out the noun on the right which is not used with the verb on the left.

4 marks

1 make   homework / friends / a meal / a noise *a noise research* — *mistake*
2 have   a drink / a bath / a party / a noise
3 take   photos / research / a decision / a train
4 do   a mistake / a course / someone a favour / housework

19.4 Rewrite these sentences starting with the words you are given, and without changing the meaning.

4 marks

1 I want something to eat.
  I'm ...*hungry*... .
2 I want something to drink.
  I'm ...*thirsty*... .
3 I didn't know she was pregnant.
  I didn't know she was going ...*birth*... .
4 I really enjoyed Brazil.
  I had a great ...*time in Brasil*...

Give, keep, break, catch, see

20.1

16 marks

Complete the sentences below with a verb from box A and a noun from box B.

A
break	give
keep	catch

B
train	hand	ball	record
hands	glasses	law	cold

1 I need a bit of help with this thing. Could you possibly _give_ me a _hand_ ?
2 It's too far to walk. Why don't we _catch_ the _train_ ? They run every few minutes, so we shouldn't have to wait long.
3 Why don't you wear these gloves? They'll _keep_ your _hands_ warm.
4 I think I _caught_ a _cold_ yesterday because I've been sneezing all morning, I've got a sore throat, and I feel terrible.
5 Everyone _breaks_ the _law_ at some time in their lives. For most people it is driving above the speed limit or parking illegally.
✗6 I _keep_ breaking _glasses_ . Last week I smashed three, and soon we won't have anything to drink out of.
7 She threw the _ball_ to me and I tried to _catch_ it. Unfortunately I dropped it and I also hurt my finger.
8 We have to be careful with money, so we _keep_ a _record_ of everything we spend and write it down in this book.

20.2

8 marks

Complete the phrases in *italics*.

1 If you *keep* _in_ _touch_ *with someone*, it means you remember to write to or phone them on a regular basis.
2 If you say something to _break_ *the* _ice_ , it means you say something to make people feel more relaxed in a situation when they first meet you and other strangers for the first time.
3 If someone says to you, *please* _give_ *my* _regard_ *to Jane*, it means they want you to say 'hello' to Jane when you see her (because they can't).
4 If you say that you don't *see the* _point_ _of_ *doing something*, it means you don't see any reason to do it. It just seems a stupid thing to do.

20.3

6 marks

Complete these dialogues with a suitable verb.

1 A: What shall we do if they can't take our order?
  B: I don't know. I'll _see_ what John says.
2 A: Put this coat on – it'll _keep_ you dry if it rains.
  B: Thanks.
3 A: If you put the white next to the yellow, the white looks dirty.
  B: Yes, I _see_ what you mean.
4 A: He only needs to play for England three more times and he'll _break_ the record.
  B: I know. It's fantastic.
5 A: I'll _give_ you a ring about eight.
  B: Could you phone a bit later? I'll be having dinner at eight.
6 A: What's the matter?
  B: I don't know but I _keep_ getting headaches. I think I should make an appointment to see the doctor.

21 Get: uses and expressions

21.1
10 marks

Match the word *get* in sentences in 1–10 with the meanings in the diagram. There are two sentences for each meaning.

~~function inform~~

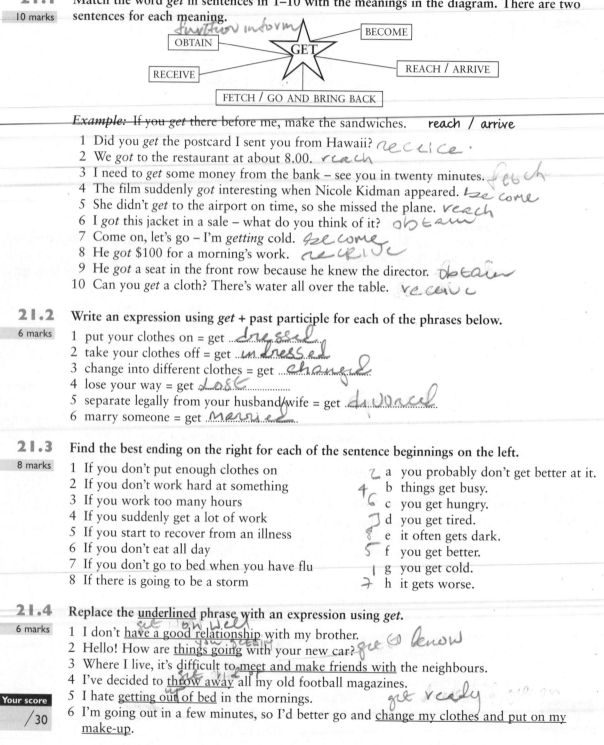

OBTAIN · BECOME · GET · RECEIVE · REACH / ARRIVE · FETCH / GO AND BRING BACK

Example: If you *get* there before me, make the sandwiches.   reach / arrive

1 Did you *get* the postcard I sent you from Hawaii? ~~receive~~
2 We *got* to the restaurant at about 8.00. ~~reach~~
3 I need to *get* some money from the bank – see you in twenty minutes. ~~fetch~~
4 The film suddenly *got* interesting when Nicole Kidman appeared. ~~become~~
5 She didn't *get* to the airport on time, so she missed the plane. ~~reach~~
6 I *got* this jacket in a sale – what do you think of it? ~~obtain~~
7 Come on, let's go – I'm *getting* cold. ~~become~~
8 He *got* $100 for a morning's work. ~~receive~~
9 He *got* a seat in the front row because he knew the director. ~~obtain~~
10 Can you *get* a cloth? There's water all over the table. ~~receive~~

21.2
6 marks

Write an expression using *get* + past participle for each of the phrases below.

1 put your clothes on = get .....dressed.....
2 take your clothes off = get .....undressed.....
3 change into different clothes = get .....changed.....
4 lose your way = get .....lost.....
5 separate legally from your husband/wife = get .....divorced.....
6 marry someone = get .....married.....

21.3
8 marks

Find the best ending on the right for each of the sentence beginnings on the left.

1 If you don't put enough clothes on   2 a you probably don't get better at it.
2 If you don't work hard at something   4 b things get busy.
3 If you work too many hours   6 c you get hungry.
4 If you suddenly get a lot of work   3 d you get tired.
5 If you start to recover from an illness   8 e it often gets dark.
6 If you don't eat all day   5 f you get better.
7 If you don't go to bed when you have flu   1 g you get cold.
8 If there is going to be a storm   7 h it gets worse.

21.4
6 marks

Replace the <u>underlined phrase</u> with an expression using *get*.

1 I don't <u>have a good relationship</u> with my brother. ~~get on well~~
2 Hello! How are <u>things going</u> with your new car? ~~get on~~ ~~get to know~~
3 Where I live, it's difficult to <u>meet and make friends with</u> the neighbours.
4 I've decided to <u>throw away</u> all my old football magazines. ~~get rid of~~
5 I hate <u>getting out of bed</u> in the mornings. ~~get ready~~
6 I'm going out in a few minutes, so I'd better go and <u>change my clothes and put on my make-up</u>.

Your score
/30

24   *Test your English Vocabulary in Use (pre-intermediate and intermediate)*

Go: uses and expressions

22.1

6 marks

Complete the dialogues with a suitable adjective.

1 You'll have to shout when you speak to her; she's going ...*deaf*... .
2 I'm losing my hair, and I don't want to go ...*bald*... before I'm 40!
3 The business is losing money. I hope we don't go *bankrupt*
4 I've broken Dad's computer. He'll go ...*mad*... when he finds out.
5 I love to see the leaves go ...*blue*... in the autumn.
6 My hair was black in my twenties, but now I'm going a bit ...*grey*... .

22.2

8 marks

Look at the pictures and write sentences to describe what the couple are doing this weekend, using *go + -ing* or *go (out) for a* + noun. Sometimes both are possible.

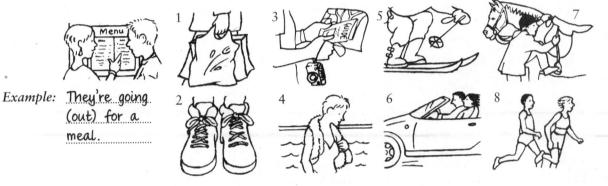

Example: They're going (out) for a meal.

22.3

7 marks

Match the answers on the right with the questions on the left.

1 Have you ever been windsurfing?
2 How fast does it go?
3 How's it going?
4 Does this road go to Brighton?
5 This train goes to London, right?
6 Is it my go?
7 Will your dad be angry about this?

5 a No, you have to change here!
7 b Yes, he'll probably go mad!
6 c I think you're after Martha.
1 d No, but I'd love to have a go.
3 e Fine, thanks. I'm enjoying it.
2 f Oh, only about 50 kph.
4 g Yes, but the motorway is quicker.

22.4

9 marks

A teacher is being interviewed at her school at the end of the day. Complete the interview using the verbs in the box in the correct form.

go	come	take	being

When I (1) ...*come*... here at 8.00 in the morning, I often (2) ...*take*... my breakfast with me and eat it here in the classroom before the children arrive. When they (3) ...*come*... in at 9.00, it's incredibly noisy at first, but they quieten down, and we work hard for about two hours. At break time, I (4) ...*take*... them to the playing field where they run about. At lunchtime, some mothers (5) ...*come*... and (6) ...*take*... their children home for an hour, but most children stay here. Quite often in the afternoons, another teacher and I (7) ...*take*... the children out on a visit. After school, my husband (8) ...*come*... and gets me in the car. I never (9) ...*go*... home until I've prepared everything for the next day.

23.1

8 marks

Complete these different ways of saying sorry in the following situations. You will need one or two words for each gap.

1 I'm really sorry *I'm* .... late.
2 Was that your foot I stepped on? I *beg* .... your pardon.
3 I'm sorry to .... *keep* .... you waiting, but I won't be .... *long* .... now.
4 I must .. *apologise* ..... for .. *being* .... late.
5 Dear Mr Patterson
   Please .. *accept* ..... our .. *apologies* ... for the mistake in your order. Unfortunately you received equipment that should have gone to an address in London, and ...

23.2

8 marks

Write correct responses in each of the situations below, using the words in the box (in the correct form), and starting with the words you are given.

| sort something out   cancel   delay   clear something up |

1 A: Were they held up?
  B: Yes, they .. *delay* ....
2 A: This room is very untidy.
  B: It's OK, I ....
3 A: Can we do anything about these problems?
  B: Yes, we can .. *sort something out* .
4 A: I thought they were having a meeting yesterday.
  B: They were, but several people were ill so they had to .. *cancel* ....

23.3

4 marks

Here are four different ways of reassuring people. Complete each phrase with a single word.

A: I'm terribly sorry.
B: That's OK. Don't .. *worry* ....
   Never .. *mind* ....
   It doesn't .. *matter* ....
   No ....

23.4

8 marks

There is one word missing in each of A's lines in this dialogue. Put the word at the end of the line and show where it goes in the line with an arrow like this (↑).

Example: A: Thank you ↑ coming to see me.   *for*
          B: No problem.

1 A: I'm really sorry the mess in here.   *about*
  B: What happened?
2 A: I spilt some coffee, but it's OK, I'll clear it. ↑   *up*
  B: Do you want some help?
3 A: Well, that's very kind you, but I can do it.   *of*
  B: OK. Shall I post these letters for you, then?
4 A: Oh, thanks lot.   *a lot*

23.5

2 marks

Your score

/30

Complete the last word in this text. The first letter of the answer is given.

You visit another country where you meet people who are very kind to you. They look after you and take you out. At the end of your stay you thank them for their h.. *hospitality*

Requests, invitations and suggestions

24.1
15 marks

Expand the notes into correct sentences by adding *one more word* after each slash (/). Look at the example first.

Example: A: Can I take / ~~this~~ chair?
B: Yes, go / *ahead*.

1 A: Could / I borrow / *you* pen / *for* five minutes?
B: Yes, / *help* yourself.

2 A: Could / *you* give / that book / *to* there?
B: Yes, / *of* course. Here you are.

3 A: I / *was* wondering / *if* I / *could* use your bike for half an hour?
B: Well, I / *d* rather/ *you* didn't actually. I may need it myself.

4 A: Do you / you could / lend / some CDs?
B: I / I could, but I haven't got any.

5 A: Mary, / you like / go / this evening?
B: I / love / but I'm / I can't.

6 A: Would you / if I / the afternoon off? I don't feel very well.
B: No, please do go home.

7 A: Can / give / a hand?
B: I / afraid / , just at the moment. I have / go out.

24.2
5 marks

Complete these dialogues by writing one or two words in each gap.

1 A: Why don't we buy her a new suitcase for her holiday?
B: Yes, *that's* a good idea.

2 A: Do you want to go and buy one now?
B: Yes, *if* you like.

3 A: Do you want the blue one?
B: I don't *mind* . You choose.

4 A: OK, let's have the blue one. It's £60 – that's £30 each.
B: You won't believe this, but I haven't got any money *on* me at all.

5 A: I'll lend you the money. You can give it back to me tonight.
B: I'm *sorry* , but I won't be able to get to the bank by then. Is tomorrow OK?

24.3
10 marks

Replace the underlined words and phrases using words from the box. Add, change or remove any other words to make the English grammatically correct.

how about	I'd prefer	evening	mind	shall

1 A: What *shall we do* <u>do you want to</u> do at the weekend?
2 B: Uh, let me think. OK, <u>why don't we go</u> to the beach? *How about going to the bea...*
3 A: Yeah, great. And <u>tonight</u>? Do you want to see that film?
4 B: I think <u>I'd rather</u> *prefer* stay in, actually. *this evening*
5 A: Yes, OK, <u>that's fine with me</u>. *I don't mind*

Your score
/30

25 Opinions, agreeing and disagreeing

25.1 Find eight mistakes in this dialogue and correct them.
8 marks

A: What do you think for this idea to stop free eye tests?
B: I think it's not a good idea. In my meaning, people will just stop going to the optician's.
C: I'm afraid but I total disagree.
A: Yes, it's written in one newspaper that most people are happy to pay for an eye test.
B: You can be right, but don't you think it's more complicated than that?
C: Yes, I'm agree, that's true.

25.2 Organise sentences a–f into a logical dialogue.
6 marks

a As far as I'm concerned, that's long enough.
b Yes, you could be right about education, but don't forget they've only been in power for six months.
c Why's that?
d How do you feel about the new government?
e Well, I don't think they've done much to improve schools.
f Personally I don't think they're any better than the last one.

25.3 Rewrite the sentences using the word on the right. Start with the words you are given. The
10 marks meaning must stay the same.

1 What do you think of his new plan?
What _are you feeling about his new plan_? FEELINGS
2 Well, in my opinion, more people should go to university.
Well, _as far as I'm concerned more people should go to u_ CONCERNED
3 You know, the paper says he is still missing.
You know, _according the paper says he's still missing_ ACCORDING
4 I agree with you.
I _think your right,_ RIGHT
5 I partly agree with you.
I _agree with you some extent,_ EXTENT

25.4 Complete the dialogue with suitable phrases.
6 marks

A: (1) _What is your honest_ of the new underground system here?
B: Well, (2) _Personally_, I find it quite comfortable and quick.
A: I (3) _agree_ that it's quick, but it does seem a bit expensive.
B: I agree with you to (4) _a certain extent_ but it's still cheaper than in many countries.
A: Really? But (5) _according_ the newspapers, this government doesn't spend nearly enough on public transport.
B: I'm sorry, but I just (6) _can't believe that's_ true.

26 Specific situations and special occasions

26.1
6 marks

Look at the words and phrases in bold in the following dialogues. Are they correct or incorrect? If there is a mistake, correct it.

1 In a restaurant. It's 8pm:
    A: **Goodnight** *evening* sir. Have you reserved a table?
    B: Yes, a table for four. The name's Robson.

2 Meeting someone for the first time:
    A: How do you do? *Pleased to meet you*
    B: **Fine, thank you.**

3 To someone on their birthday:
    A: **Many happy returns.**
    B: Thank you.

4 In the office on Friday afternoon:
    A: Have a nice weekend.
    B: **Yes, same for you.** *to*

5 Saying goodbye to a friend:
    A: Bye. See you soon.
    B: Bye.

6 Speaking to a friend:
    A: Oh, no! I've failed my exam again!
    B: Oh, **hard luck.**

26.2
8 marks

Complete these explanations. Each gap represents one word.

1 We often say '_Good_ _luck_' to wish people well before an exam.
2 When we have an alcoholic drink with friends (especially the first one), we sometimes hold up our glasses and say '_cheers_' before we start drinking.
3 We often say '_bless_ _you_' to people when they sneeze and they can answer by saying '_thank_ _you_'.
4 When we want to get past someone in a crowded place we usually say '_excuse_ _me_, please.'
5 When someone wants to warn or tell you about a danger or an accident that might happen, they shout '_watch_ out!'
6 If you don't know the answer to something, you can say, 'I've no _idea_.'
7 On January 1st, in many countries people say '_happy_ _new_ Year.'

26.3
4 marks

Find another way to say the expressions on the left.

1 You passed. Congratulations!   You passed. Well _done_!
2 Goodbye. Nice to meet you.   Goodbye. Nice to have _met you_.
3 That's your coat. I'm very sorry.   That's your coat. I beg your _pardon_.
4 Hi. How are you?   Hi. How's it _going_?

26.4
12 marks

True or false? If an answer is false, change it to make it true.

1 When we meet people for the first time in a formal situation we can say **How do you do?** or **How are you?**
2 When people say **How are you?** a common response is **Not bad. How about you?**
3 Cheerio is another way of saying 'Hello'. *afternoon*
4 When we go to bed we often say **Goodnight** to other people.
5 We can say **Sorry** if we don't hear what someone says and we want them to repeat it.
6 British people say **Good morning** up to lunchtime, but in the afternoon they say **Good day.**
7 The French say **Bon appetit** before a meal, but there isn't a similar expression in English.
8 To wish someone well at Christmas or on their birthday, we can say **Merry Christmas** or **Merry Birthday.** *Happy*

27 Uncountable nouns and plural nouns

27.1 Are these rules true or false? If they are false, correct them.

5 marks

1 Nouns like *information* and *furniture* cannot be counted in English, so they don't have a plural form with 's' on the end. ✓
2 These nouns are used with a singular verb (e.g. *is* not *are*). ✓
3 They cannot be used with the definite article *the*. ✗
4 The words *trousers*, *clothes* and *pyjamas* always have 's' on the end. ✓
5 They are used with a singular verb. ✗

27.2 Circle the correct answer.

6 marks

1 I couldn't get all the (information) / informations I needed.
2 She doesn't have a work / (any work) at the moment.
3 We had (good weather) / a good weather.
4 I definitely need a new trousers / (a new pair of trousers).
5 (My hair is) / my hairs are very dry at the moment.
6 Have you done the (housework) / houseworks?

27.3 Rewrite these sentences. Start with the words you are given and include the words on the right. The meaning must stay the same.

12 marks

1 I don't usually take many suitcases with me.
I don't usually take ~~luggage with me~~   LUGGAGE
2 Her teacher sometimes gives her a lot of things to do in the evening.
Her teacher sometimes gives her ~~homework to do~~   HOMEWORK
3 She's definitely getting better.
She's definitely ~~making progress~~   PROGRESS
4 He gave me a lot of ideas.
He gave me ~~a lot of advice~~   ADVICE
5 I only know a few words of Spanish.
I only ~~have little knowledge of Spanish~~   KNOWLEDGE
6 I'm going to buy some jeans.
I'm going to buy ~~pair of jeans~~   PAIR

27.4 Label these nouns.

7 marks

1 ~~Sunglasses~~ 2 ~~Short~~   3 ~~Scales~~   4 ~~scissors~~

5 ~~stairs~~   6 ~~pyjamas~~   7 ~~Headphones~~

Your score
/30

Test your English Vocabulary in Use (pre-intermediate and intermediate)

28 Verbs + -ing form or infinitive

28.1 Are these verbs followed by the *-ing* form or the infinitive?
8 marks

finish ✓   refuse ✓   avoid ✓   seem
hope   imagine ✓ decide ✓ admit ✓

28.2 Circle the correct answers. There are two in each question.
6 marks

1 He .... going out at night.
   a) *enjoys*   b) can't stand   c) wants
2 They .... to finish work at 7.00.
   a) imagined   b) expected   c) *managed*
3 I .... to work on Sunday.
   a) *decided*   b) felt like   c) offered
4 Would you .... to help him?
   a) avoid   b) refuse   c) *promise*
5 She .... to go to the bank.
   a) meant   b) *forgot*   c) didn't mind
6 She .... to know a lot about computers.
   a) seems   b) denies   c) *wants*

28.3 Complete the definitions below with the correct verb from the box.
8 marks

allow	remember	can't stand	manage
let	make	deny	give up

1 If you ....*give up*.... doing something, it means you stop doing it.
2 If you ....*can't*.... doing something, it means you hate doing it.
3 If you ....*manage*.... to do something, it means you do it, but it isn't easy.
4 If you ....*deny*.... doing something, it means you say that you didn't do it.
5 If you ....*make*.... someone do something, it means you tell or force them to do it.
6 If you ....*remember*.... to do something, it means you don't forget to do it.
7 If you ....*let*.... someone do something, it means that you permit them to do it.
8 If you ....*allow*.... someone to do something, it means that you permit them to do it.

28.4 Rewrite the sentences using the two words on the right. Add, change or remove any other words to make the English grammatically correct.
8 marks

Example: I said I would go in ten minutes, but he made me go immediately.
   I *promised to go in ten minutes but he forced me*   PROMISE / FORCE
   to go immediately.

1 He likes playing football, but he doesn't think he will get a place on the team.
   He *enjoys playing football, but he doesn't expect to get*   ENJOY / EXPECT
2 He says he took the money, but he says he didn't hit the guard.
   He *admits taking money, but he denies hit the guard.*   ADMIT / DENY
3 She will help us today, but she isn't prepared to come tomorrow.
   She's *offer us to help but she's refused to come tomorrow*   OFFER / REFUSE
4 I would like to go out, but my parents won't allow me to use the car.
   I *feel like to go out, but my parents won't let me*   FEEL LIKE / LET

Your score
/30

Verb patterns

29.1

6 marks

Match the verbs in the box with the correct definition below.

blame   complain   warn   insist   apologise   persuade

1 demand something strongly *4*
2 successfully change someone's opinion about something *6*
3 hold someone responsible for something that goes wrong *1*
4 say sorry *5*
5 tell someone of a possible danger *3*
6 say you are not happy or satisfied with something *2*

29.2

12 marks

Report these sentences, starting with the verbs you are given. Make any changes that are necessary, but the meaning must stay the same. In each sentence the speaker is talking to *you*.

1 'The course was a waste of time.'
She told *me the course is had been a waste of time.*
2 'Could you leave by the side door?'
She asked *me to leave by the side door.*
3 'I think you should buy another one.'
She advised *me to buy another one.*
4 'Why don't we do the exercise later?'
She suggested *me doing the exercise later.*
5 'Please don't go near the rocks.'
She warned *me not to go near the rocks.*
6 'Don't tell anyone.'
She insisted *that I don't tell anyone.*

29.3

8 marks

Is the <u>underlined</u> word in these sentences correct? If not, cross it out.

1 She said <u>me</u> it was a great idea.
2 He explained <u>me</u> what to do.
3 They told <u>us</u> there were dangerous animals in the fields.
4 One of them suggested <u>us</u> a picnic.
5 I persuaded <u>them</u> to leave.
6 The hotel confirmed <u>us</u> our reservation for the weekend.
7 She proposed <u>us</u> a very interesting new plan.
8 They wanted <u>me</u> to stay.

29.4

4 marks

Complete these sentences with a preposition.

1 She blamed him *for*
the accident.

2 He insisted *on*
paying for the damage.

3 She apologised *for*
shouting at him.

4 They complained *about*
the faulty traffic lights.

Test your English Vocabulary in Use (pre-intermediate and intermediate)

30.1
10 marks

Scale adjectives talk about degree e.g. *good – quite good – very good*; limit adjectives describe extremes e.g. *marvellous – absolutely marvellous*. You cannot say *absolutely good* or *very marvellous*. Complete the table with suitable adjectives.

'Scale' adjectives	'Limit' adjectives	'Scale' adjectives	'Limit' adjectives
bad	terrible, awful	good	marvellous
big	huge, enormous	*crowded*	packed
interesting	*fascinating*	small	*tiny*
surprised	*astonished, amazed*	*hungry*	starving
hot	boiling	tired	*exhausted*
cold	*freezing*	frightened	*terrified*

30.2
6 marks

Complete the sentences using a suitable limit adjective.

1 A: How was the football match?
   B: OK, but it was ...*packed*... – there were so many people we couldn't really see.
2 We didn't get a meal till 9.00 and I was absolutely ...*starving*...
3 A: How's your new office?
   B: Oh, the temperature's awful. It's either ...*freezing*... or absolutely ...*boiling*...
4 Our holiday villa was ...*huge*...; it slept 12 easily.
5 The new disco is absolutely ...*terrible*... I'd never go there again – I hated it.

30.3
9 marks

Circle the correct answer.

1 We had a terrific/(terrifying) time in the mountains – I'm not going back there again.
2 The food was so (terrific)/terrible that we wrote to thank the manager and chef.
3 She had to pay a great/(huge) bill at the end of the holiday.
4 He came out of the women's toilet with a red face looking really confused/(embarrassed).
5 The children loved the zoo and came home really (excited)/astonished.
6 I was surprising/(astonished) that she didn't pass her exam.
7 We had a nice day, but the weather was (absolutely)/very dreadful.
8 The trip was very (boring)/tiring but we enjoyed it a lot.
9 The wildlife film was really fascinated/(fascinating).

30.4
5 marks

Rewrite the sentences using the word on the right. Start with the words you are given. The meaning must stay the same.

1 I'm disappointed in her results.
   Her ...*results were disappointing*...   DISAPPOINTING
2 I found the map very confusing.
   I ...*was confused by the map*...   CONFUSED
3 I was depressed by the sales figures.
   The ...*sales figures was depressing*...   DEPRESSING
4 The film she saw was really frightening.
   She ...*was really frightened by the film*...   FRIGHTENED
5 I was exhausted by the climb.
   The ...*climb was exhausting*...   EXHAUSTING

Your score

/30

31 Prepositions: place

31.1

10 marks

Correct any mistakes with prepositions in these sentences. Be careful: some are correct.

1 She doesn't live in London any longer.
2 The food is in the table. *on*
3 I'm just going to make a phone call but I'll see you on work. *at*
4 Don't put those books on the floor.
5 We're staying at a very nice area. *in*
6 They should be in the party tonight if you want to see them. *at*
7 Put the keys at your pocket. *in*
8 I said I'd see her at the end of the road.
9 I always sit in the table for dinner. *at*
10 We can play on the garden. *in*

31.2

10 marks

Complete the sentences below.

1 **Down the stairs** is the opposite of ....*up*.... **the stairs**.
2 **Into the room** is the opposite of ...*out of*... **the room**.
3 **We drove under the bridge** is the opposite of **we drove** ...*over*... **the bridge**.
4 **We flew above the clouds** is the opposite of **we flew** ...*below*... **the clouds**.
5 **In front of the school** is the opposite of ...*out of*... **the school**.

Complete these sentences with the correct preposition/prepositional phrase from above.

6 The money fell ...*up*... my pocket.
7 If you stand ...*in front of*... me, I can't see the picture.
8 The cat was frightened and ran ...*up*... that tree over there.
9 I'm on the top floor and at the moment the flat ...*below*... me is empty.
10 We are going to fly ...*over*... the city and then land at the airport.

31.3

10 marks

Complete these sentences with suitable prepositions.

1 I ran ...*towards*... the house but stopped when I saw a big dog.

2 John came over and sat ...*besides*... me.

3 Ten minutes later Rosa joined us and sat down ...*between*... us.

4 I'm sure the post office is just ...*opposite*... the bank.

5 The cat suddenly ran ...*across*... the road. It must have seen something on the other side.

6 We walked along the road, ...*past*... a church and then came to a park.
7 They must have walked ...*beside*... the river for about five miles.
8 We wanted to go ...*through*... the town using the bypass, but we never saw the road, so we had to drive right ...*near*... the middle of the town.
9 The station is quite ...*near*... here: about a ten-minute walk at the most, I'd say.

Your score

/30

Test your English Vocabulary in Use (pre-intermediate and intermediate)

32 Adverbs: frequency and degree

32.1
7 marks

Do the words in *italics* have the same meaning in these sentences? Write *Yes* or *No*.

1 It *rarely/seldom* rains here during the summer.
2 We *regularly/hardly ever* go to the local sports centre.
3 We see that couple *frequently/occasionally* in the park.
4 It's an *incredibly/extremely* expensive restaurant, but the food is fantastic.
5 They *seldom/ never* go out after 10.00 o'clock in the evening.
6 I thought she was getting *slightly/a bit* fatter.
7 Come on! It's *nearly/almost* time to go.

32.2
4 marks

Put the following adverbs in order of frequency on the line.

hardly ever	occasionally	regularly	sometimes

100% of the time   0%
ALWAYS   NEVER

32.3
5 marks

Organise the words into correct sentences. Sometimes more than one answer is possible.

1 hardly is ever he work for late
2 children we the take pool occasionally to the
3 has hotel she stayed same the always in
4 forget lock quite I the often door to
5 rarely find you fresh in can market fish the

32.4
7 marks

Circle the correct answer.

1 Which is more informal? <u>We were a bit tired.</u> / <u>We were fairly tired.</u>
2 Which is more positive? <u>It was pretty good.</u> / <u>It was quite good.</u>
3 In which sentence is the speaker more surprised? <u>The film was quite interesting.</u> / <u>The film was rather interesting.</u>
4 Which is more informal? <u>We had quite a good time.</u> / <u>We had a pretty good time.</u>
5 Which is more negative? <u>I find it slightly boring.</u> / <u>I find it quite boring.</u>
6 Which is not correct? <u>It's almost the same as yours.</u> / <u>It's quite the same as yours.</u>
7 Which is more formal? <u>I hardly ever see him.</u> / <u>I seldom see him.</u>

32.5
7 marks

What is the correct place in the sentence for the words on the right? Show your answer with an arrow like this. (↑)

1 There was enough room to sit down in the departure lounge.	HARDLY
2 It happened so quickly, we had time to think.	BARELY
3 It was dark before the repair man arrived.	ALMOST
4 We were tired after travelling so far that day.	INCREDIBLY
5 Her father forgot to give her the money for the shopping.	NEARLY
6 I was shocked to hear she had got married again.	A BIT
7 His brother comes to see me these days.	HARDLY EVER

Your score
/30

33 Time and sequence

33.1

12 marks

Circle the correct answer(s). There is sometimes more than one.

1 I'll let you know _when_ I've made my decision.
   a) when   b) while   c) as soon as
2 Pete cleaned the kitchen _while_ I did the living room.
   a) when   b) while   c) as soon as
3 We heard the noise _when_ we were getting ready.
   a) when   b) while   c) as soon as
4 I got to the gallery _as_ it was closing.
   a) as   b) while   c) just as
5 It'll get warmer in here _while_ the heating comes on.
   a) when   b) while   c) as soon as
6 I met them _when_ I was in New York.
   a) when   b) while   c) just as
7 We made the dinner _while_ John wrote his essay.
   a) when   b) while   c) just as

33.2

4 marks

Complete this sequence of actions with suitable link words or phrases. Do not use any single word or phrase more than once.

A: What did you do for your holiday this year?
B: Well, (1) _first of all_ we took the train up to Edinburgh and spent a couple of nights there. (2) _then_ we hired a car and travelled round Scotland for about five days. (3) _After that_ we took the train right the way down to the south coast where we stayed with relatives for a few days; and (4) _finally_ we came back to London in their car and showed them round for a couple of days. It was very nice.

33.3

6 marks

Read this short text, then answer the questions below.

First, we took the wrong turning and ended up in the middle of an industrial estate. **Then** we got lost and drove round in circles for half an hour **before we found** the right road. But we got there **in the end,** and had a very nice meal at their house. **After that** we all went on to a club.

1 Could you use 'firstly' in place of 'first'? ✓
2 Could you say 'before finding' in place of 'before we found'? ✓
3 Could you say 'before to find' in place of 'before we found'? ✗
4 Could you say 'besides' in place of 'in the end'? ✗
5 Could you say 'eventually' in place of 'in the end'? ✓
6 Could you say 'afterwards' in place of 'after that'? ✓

33.4

8 marks

Fill the gaps in these dialogues with a single word.

1 A: Why is it so cold in here?
   B: Well, for one _for one thing_ the heating isn't on; and for _another_ thing, someone has left the door open.
2 A: Why don't we finish the letters and send them off?
   B: Well, to _start_ with, we really need Patricia's help with one or two. And _anyway_, we haven't got the addresses, so we can't send them.

Your score

/30

Test your English Vocabulary in Use (pre-intermediate and intermediate)

Addition and contrast

34.1

10 marks

Use the words and phrases in the box to complete the sentences below.

however	furthermore	as well	although	whereas

1 They're completely different: James wants to go out and play in any kind of weather, ~~whereas~~ the twins are happy to stay at home and play on the computer.
2 I was expecting a present. I didn't know they were organising a party for me ~~as well~~.
3 It was quite a nice place, ~~although~~ the streets were rather dirty.
4 Mandy was very keen to go to the party. Her sister Carol, ~~furthermore~~, preferred to stay at home.
5 We advise our clients to rent the apartment on the top floor as it is much quieter. ~~furthermore~~ it has the advantage of the best view of any of the flats.

Now write down an alternative word or phrase that would also be correct in each of the sentences 1–5 above.

6 (sentence 1) ~~while~~
7 (sentence 2) ~~too~~
8 (sentence 3) ~~even though~~ ~~but~~

9 (sentence 4) ~~on the other hand~~
10 (sentence 5) ~~also, in addition~~ ~~moreover, what's more~~

34.2

8 marks

Choose the ending which is logical and grammatically correct in these sentences.

1 We stayed in that hotel despite ~~the noise~~ .
   a) the good food   b) it was expensive   c) the noise ✓   d) it was near
2 Most of us thought it was great. Peter, on the other hand, ~~hated it~~ .
   a) loved it   b) hated it ✓   c) agreed   d) was very happy
3 With this ticket you can go and come back when you want. What's more, ~~it's very cheap~~
   a) it's very expensive   b) it's very cheap ✓   c) other tickets are better value
4 He went to the meeting in spite of ~~feeling ill~~ .
   a) feeling ill ✓   b) feel ill   c) to feel ill
5 He bought that watch even though ~~he wanted it~~
   a) he wanted it   b) having one already   c) it was expensive
6 The first test was extremely hard, whereas ~~a~~ .
   a) the second was easy   b) I passed   c) the second was more difficult
7 My new house is big and very light. In addition, ~~b~~ .
   a) it's a bit expensive   b) it's near a lovely park   c) there isn't much space
8 I forgot to send them a map. However, ~~a~~ .
   a) they still found the house easily   b) they got lost   c) I forgot to phone them.

34.3

12 marks

Fill the gaps in this text with suitable link words or phrases.

By the time we set up camp on the second day there were already tensions between us. I was exhausted and wanted to stop, (1) ~~while~~ Pete wanted to continue for another four or five miles. (2) ~~However~~ , after a bit of an argument, we did decide to stop at this point and pitch our tents. We managed to do this (3) ~~despite~~ the hard ground and a strong wind. The atmosphere between us was really quite unpleasant. (4) ~~What's more~~ we were worried about the weather, which was getting worse. Anyway, I built a fire and starting preparing dinner. Pete, (5) ~~on the other hand~~, decided he'd had enough and went off to find a pub serving hot food. We never spoke to each other again (6) ~~although~~ we worked in the same office for another six months.

Test your English Vocabulary in Use (pre-intermediate and intermediate)

35 Similarities, differences and conditions

35.1

7 marks

Look at the pictures, then complete the sentences below using the phrases in the box. Use each phrase once only.

Anne   Barbara   Claire   Diana

except that	quite alike	neither	very different
quite unlike	similar	both	

1 Anne is ....Similar........... to Barbara.
2 Diana and Claire are ...quite alike.. .
3 Barbara is ...quite unlike. Claire.
4 Anne is ..very d........... from Diana, ...except....... they ....both............. have wavy hair.
5 ...Neither....... Anne nor Barbara has short hair.

35.2

10 marks

Make five correct and logical sentences using words and phrases from each column. You cannot use a word or phrase more than once.

1 You'll lose your umbrella   OTHERWISE   a you're wearing glasses.
2 I think you'll pass the test   IN CASE   b you keep it in your bag.
3 You'd better take some money   AS LONG AS   c you don't get too nervous.
4 You should leave by 7.00   UNLESS   d you have to take a taxi.
5 You look the same as usual   EXCEPT THAT   e you'll miss the bus.

35.3

8 marks

Do the underlined phrases have the same meaning or a different meaning?

1 David and his brother have a lot in common / similar interests.
2 They made a comparison of / They compared the cost of living in their countries.
3 Alan and Carole both hate / Neither Alan nor Carole hate cleaning the house.
4 I'll go to the library if / unless it rains.
5 Everyone arrived on time apart from / except for Lucy.
6 Hedda and her brother are quite alike. / Hedda quite likes her brother.
7 I'll work on Sunday as long as / on condition that I get paid overtime.
8 I'll take my coat in case / if it's cold.

35.4

5 marks

Complete these sentences with a suitable word or phrase.

1 We get on well, although we have ....nothing........... in common.
2 London is very big ..in comparison..with my home town.
3 The children were all late ....except........... Sue, who was on time.

Your score

/30

4 You'll be late ...unless............ you hurry.
5 I'd better do my homework ...otherwise........ my teacher will be angry.

36 Reason, purpose and result

36.1
Make six correct and logical sentences using words and phrases from each column. You cannot use a word or phrase more than once.

Column 1	Column 2	Column 3
1 I lost my wallet,	because of	I learnt the bad news much later.
2 I went to the post office	so that	I had to borrow some money.
3 I had to stop the traffic	Consequently,	I needed some stamps.
4 I stayed at work late	so	I have given up work to look after her.
5 My wife is very ill and	because	I could finish the report.
6 I couldn't go to the meeting.	therefore	the accident.

36.2
Choose the most logical ending for these sentences.

1 The purpose of joining the class was
   a) to improve my English.   b) that I needed English for my job.
2 A fall in sales could lead to
   a) a financial crisis in the company.   b) a pay rise for all the workers.
3 The investigators decided that the bad weather caused
   a) the ice.   b) the accident.
4 The company's economic problems have resulted in
   a) the loss of ten jobs.   b) the world's financial situation.
5 She bought the bike so that
   a) she had won some money.   b) she could get to work more cheaply.
6 The police believe the young boy was responsible for
   a) the fire.   b) his parents.

36.3
Circle the correct link word or phrase in the sentences below.

1 Due to / As it was raining heavily, we left early.
2 Owing to / Because the bad weather, the match began late.
3 A fight started. As a result / So, several people were taken to hospital.
4 The boy failed his exam because / because of his illness.
5 She parked on a busy, narrow bridge. Consequently / Owing to, she was fined £50.
6 They gave him a medal since / because of his bravery.
7 We got a taxi because / because of we were late.

36.4
Complete the sentences below using the correct word or phrase from the box.

consequently	so that	and therefore	as	due to

1 We've decided to move house ......as...... my wife has a new job in London.
2 Many visitors to the hotel have complained about the bathrooms. Consequently, we intend to decorate them all this year.
3 The plane was delayed ...due to... the foggy weather.
4 My parents are unwell ...and therefore... I have decided to move nearer them.
5 Bring the chairs inside ...so that... they don't get wet.

The physical world

37.1

12 marks

Complete the sentences below using words from the box.

mountain	river	desert	ocean
island	continent	jungle	group of islands
Lake	Sea	country	mountain range

1 The Balearics are a *group of islands* in the Mediterranean.
2 The Pyrenees is a *mountain* between France and Spain.
3 The Mississippi is the longest *river* in North America.
4 Crete is a Greek *island* in the Aegean.
5 The Kalahari is a *desert* in Africa.
6 *Lake* Tanganyika is between the Congo and Tanzania.
7 The Pacific is the largest *ocean* in the world.
8 Mont Blanc is the highest *mountain* in France.
9 Asia is a *continent*.
10 Japan is a *country* in the Far East.
11 The Amazon rainforest is a *jungle* in South America.
12 The Red *Sea* is in the Middle East.

37.2

6 marks

Complete the sentences.

1 The *earth* goes round the sun.
2 Niagara *falls* are on the border of Canada and the USA.
3 The North and South *Poles* are at opposite ends of the earth.
4 The *stars* shine in the sky at night.
5 The *equator* goes round the centre of the earth.
6 There is a full *moon* every 28 days.

37.3

6 marks

Put the article 'the' where necessary.

1 .... Lake Titikaka   3 *The* Sahara Desert   5 *The* Black Forest
2 .... Mount Fuji   4 *The* Atlantic Ocean   6 .... Europe

37.4

6 marks

Match the words in the box with the pictures.

flood	volcanic eruption	earthquake	drought	hurricane

1 *drought* 2 *volcanic eruption* 3 *flood* 4 *earthquake hurricane*

6 The general word used to describe these five events is 'natural *disasters*'.

38.1 Complete this table.
8 marks

Noun	Adjective	Noun	Adjective
sun	*sunny*	wind	*windy*
cloud	*cloudy*	fog	*foggy*
ice		*heat*	hot
shower	*showery*	*humidity*	humid

38.2 Put the words in the first column in order from the hottest (1) to the coldest (6). Put the
5 marks words in the second column in order from the most gentle (1) to the strongest (4).

Column 1
2 — hot
4 — not very warm
6 — freezing
5 — chilly
1 — boiling
3 — warm

Column 2
2 — a wind
3 — a gale
1 — a breeze
4 — a hurricane

38.3 Complete the sentences.
6 marks
1 The weather forecast said there could be some *heavy* rain this afternoon, so you will need your coat and your umbrella.
2 In the summer it's very calm, but in the winter you can get a very *strong* wind coming off the sea.
3 I was woken up in the night by some incredible thunder and *lightning*, and I think it may have hit a tree nearby.
4 You can't go out in this weather – it's *pouring* with rain.
5 One of the weather forecasters said we would have a *spell/period* of hot weather.
6 The wind *blew* all the leaves off the trees yesterday.

38.4 Complete the sentences.
11 marks
1 It was so *foggy* that I could only see about 50 metres in front of me.
2 The car didn't stop when I put on the brakes, because the road was so *icy* .
3 They wanted to know the *temperature* so I had to go and find my thermometer.
4 They don't think it's going to rain all day, but we may get a couple of *showers* this afternoon, so take an umbrella.
5 *Hurricanes* are winds which often reach over 100 km per hour and can destroy trees and buildings quite easily.
6 It's getting very humid, and the wind is also starting to increase, so I think we could get a *humidity* quite soon.
7 We write –10 °C, but we say *minus* ten degrees centigrade, or ten degrees below *zero/freezing point*
8 It's not so bad in very hot weather if you can feel a gentle *breeze* on your face. You often get this near the sea.
9 It's really hot and unpleasant today – you know, there's 90% *humidity* .
10 There was a lot of sun this morning, but this afternoon it got quite *cloudy* and was much cooler.

Your score
/30

Test your English Vocabulary in Use (pre-intermediate and intermediate) 41

39.1 Label the drawing.

6 marks

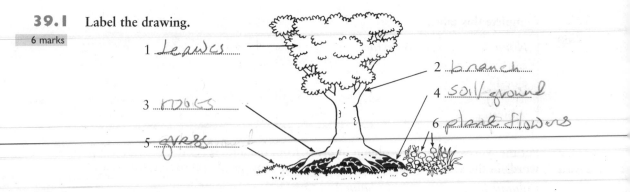

1 _leaves_

2 _branch_

4 _soil/ground_

6 _plant flowers_

3 _roots_

5 _grass_

39.2 Complete the text using the words in the box. Change the form of the word if necessary.

13 marks

pick	farm	agriculture	water
drought	keep	slaughter	plant
grow	ground	crop	harvest
dairy			

My family owns a large (1) _farm_ in the south of England. When I was 18, I studied (2) _agriculture_ at college so that I would understand farming better. My brother is in charge of one part of the business and he (3) _keeps_ cows and sheep. Some of these are (4) _slaughter_ and sold for their meat. He also sells (5) _dairy_ produce such as milk, butter and cheese. In my part of the business, we have (6) _crops_ such as maize and wheat. We (7) _grew_ vegetables for a few years, but we didn't make enough money at it, so five years ago we (8) _plant_ a lot of apple and pear trees instead. In the late summer we have extra workers to help (9) _pick_ the fruit and (10) _harvest_ the wheat.

Some years are very difficult in farming. Last year, there was no rain for two months, which caused a (11) _drought_ . The (12) _ground_ was very hard and we had to (13) _water_ the maize every week.

39.3 Complete the crossword. When you have finished, the words in the tinted box will spell another word.

11 marks

1 a soft, reddish metal used for electric wires
2 When we walk, our feet are on the ....
3 Copper, tin and iron are all ....
4 If something is ...., it is worth a lot of money.
5 a place where metals are extracted from the earth
6 a dark grey metal that is magnetic
7 a softer metal sometimes used to cover other metals
8 a whitish metal that used to be used for coins and jewellery
9 money made of metal, not paper

10 a yellow metal that used to be used for coins and jewellery: it's expensive.

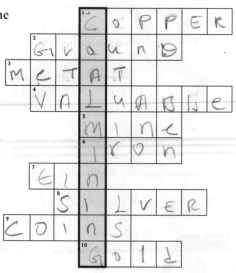

1 COPPER
2 GROUND
3 METAL
4 VALUABLE
5 MINE
6 IRON
7 TIN
8 SILVER
9 COINS
10 GOLD

Animals and insects

40.1 Label the pictures.
12 marks

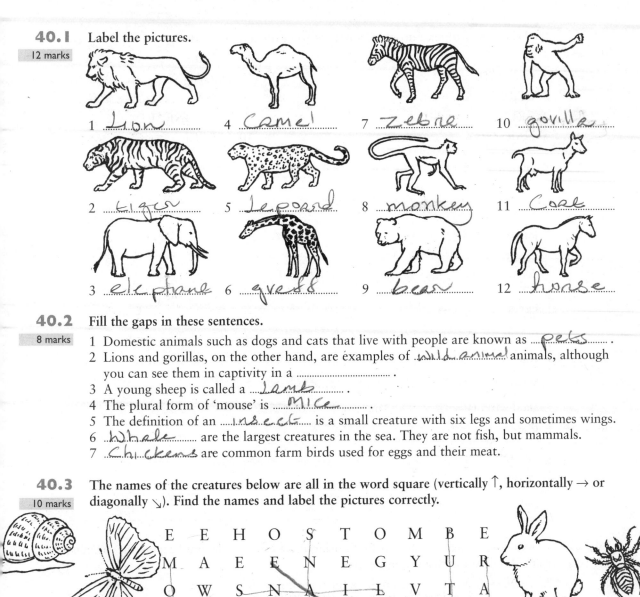

1 Lion   4 Camel   7 zebra   10 gorilla

2 tiger   5 leopard   8 monkey   11 Coat

3 elephant   6 gvess   9 bear   12 horse

40.2 Fill the gaps in these sentences.
8 marks

1 Domestic animals such as dogs and cats that live with people are known as ....pets........ .
2 Lions and gorillas, on the other hand, are examples of ...wild animal animals, although you can see them in captivity in a ....
3 A young sheep is called a ....lamb............ .
4 The plural form of 'mouse' is ...mice........... .
5 The definition of an ......insect..... is a small creature with six legs and sometimes wings.
6 ....whale........ are the largest creatures in the sea. They are not fish, but mammals.
7 ....Chickens are common farm birds used for eggs and their meat.

40.3 The names of the creatures below are all in the word square (vertically ↑, horizontally → or
10 marks diagonally ↘). Find the names and label the pictures correctly.

```
E E H O S T O M B E
M A E E N E G Y U R
O W S N A I L V T A
S H A R K G E A T B
Q U O N E Y L W E B
U N B E T F L E R I
I S P I D E R E F T
T R E E E D O B L N
O K A B T H U L Y S
```

Your score
/30

Test your English Vocabulary in Use (pre-intermediate and intermediate)

41 Countries, nationalities and languages

41.1 Find the names of ten European countries from the jumbled letters.

10 marks

1 CEFNAR _France_
2 GLORTPUA _Portugal_
3 IITRBNA _Britian_
4 KRUYET _TURKEY_
5 NARMEGY _GERMANY_

6 LTYAI _ITALY_
7 DLOAHNL _Holand_
8 PINSA _SPAIN_
9 ZLWISDNRAET _Sw_
10 EEECGR _GREECE_

41.2 Complete this table.

12 marks

Country	Nationality	Language
Japan	Japanese	
Korea	Korean	
Australia	Australian	
Egypt	Egyptian	
Brazil	Brazilian	
Argentina	Argentinian	
Sweden	Swedish	
Saudi Arabia	Arabian	
Russia	Russian	
Mexico	Mexican	
Thailand	Thai	
China	Chinese	

41.3 Rewrite the sentences below without using the word 'people' but keeping the meaning the same. Look at the two examples first.

8 marks

Examples: Russian people go there for their holidays.
  Russians go there for their holidays.
  British people work some of the longest hours in Europe.
  The British work some of the longest hours in Europe.

1 Swiss people are often multi-lingual. _The_
2 American people love baseball. _A_
3 Dutch people nearly always speak English. _The_
4 Italian people love their cars. _Italian_
5 Japanese people often take short holidays. _The Jap_
6 We do all our business with French people. _The_
7 German people go there in the summer. _G_
8 People from Israel travel a lot. _Israel_

Your score

/30

The body and what it does

42.1

13 marks

Think of a person standing up. Put the parts of the body in order from top to bottom.

neck	ankles
hips	forehead
shoulders	waist
chest	thighs
chin	lips
cheeks	eyebrows
knees	

HAIR

↓

HEELS

42.2

5 marks

Label the parts that are missing.

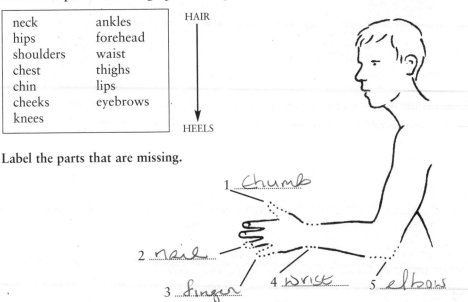

1 chumb

2 nail

3 finger   4 wrist   5 elbow

42.3

5 marks

What is the person doing in each picture? Look at the example first.

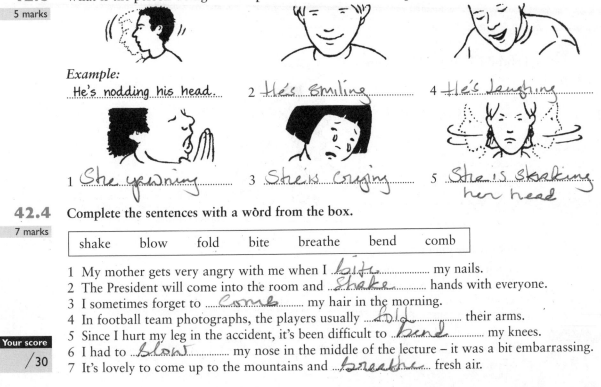

Example:
He's nodding his head.   2 He's smiling   4 He's laughing

1 She yawning   3 She is crying   5 She is shaking her head

42.4

7 marks

Complete the sentences with a word from the box.

shake	blow	fold	bite	breathe	bend	comb

1 My mother gets very angry with me when I ...bite... my nails.
2 The President will come into the room and ...shake... hands with everyone.
3 I sometimes forget to ...comb... my hair in the morning.
4 In football team photographs, the players usually ...fold... their arms.
5 Since I hurt my leg in the accident, it's been difficult to ...bend... my knees.
6 I had to ...blow... my nose in the middle of the lecture – it was a bit embarrassing.
7 It's lovely to come up to the mountains and ...breathe... fresh air.

43 Describing people's appearance

43.1 Match words from the left and right to form word partnerships. Look at the example first.

4 marks

1 hairy	a hair	hairy chest
2 blond	b chest	blond hair
3 medium	c skin	medium build
4 broad	d build	broad should
5 pale	e shoulders	pale skin

43.2 The people here would like to be the opposite of what they are. Complete the sentences.

6 marks

1 'I'm short and fat, but I'd really like to be ...... tall ...... and ... slim ....'
2 'I've got curly hair, but I've always wanted ... straight ...... hair.'
3 'I've got light brown hair, but I'd much prefer to have ...... dark ...... brown hair.'
4 'I'm rather weak, but I wish I were very strong muscul like those weightlifters and bodybuilders.'
5 'I've got a big nose, and I'm losing my hair. People don't find me attractive. Why can't I be good-looking , like Tom Cruise or Keanu Reeves?'

43.3 Find the words that have a similar meaning, then put them in the columns below to show which one in each pair has the more negative meaning.

6 marks

slim	ugly	plain	overweight	skinny	fat

Column 1   Column 2 (more negative)

Column 1	Column 2 (more negative)
slim	skinny
plain	ugly
fat	overweight

43.4 Label the features this man has.

8 marks

1 moustache

2 beard

3 a scar

4 hairy chest

43.5 Complete the dialogue.

6 marks

A: What does (1) she look like ?
B: Well, she's medium height, with long fair hair, and she always looks very elegant.
A: How (2) tall is she , exactly?
B: Oh I don't know. Probably about one metre fifty.
A: And how much (3) does she weigh
B: Well I wouldn't really like to ask that question, but I'd guess between fifty and fifty-five kilos.

Your score

/30

Test your English Vocabulary in Use (pre-intermediate and intermediate)

Describing character

44.1
6 marks

Find six pairs of words which have a similar meaning.

clever	easy-going	stupid	bright	nervous	thick
horrible	pleasant	tense	nice	relaxed	unpleasant

clever / bright   easy-going / relax

horrible / unpleasant   nervous / tense

stupid / thick   nice / pleasant

44.2
6 marks

Agree with the opinions below using a word with the same meaning. The first two letters of each answer are given.

1 A: She's always wanted to get to the top in her career, hasn't she?
   B: Yes, she's very am*bitious* .

2 A: She was horrible, wasn't she?
   B: Yes, very un*pleasant* .

3 A: He's happy and smiling whenever you see him.
   B: I know, he's always very ch*eerful* .

4 A: The problem is that she can't change any of her ideas and adapt to new ones.
   B: No, she's very in*flexible* .

5 A: Do you honestly think we can depend on that old car of yours?
   B: No, it's very un*reliable* – it could break down at any time.

6 A: He never thinks about other people's feelings, does he?
   B: No, he's very in*sensitive* .

44.3
6 marks

Write an opposite for each of these words. Three of them just require a prefix (e.g. un-; dis-); the other three need a completely different word. Look at the examples first.

Examples: happy ≠ **unhappy**   rich ≠ **poor**

1 honest   ≠ *dishonest*   4 friendly   ≠ *unfriendly*

2 generous ≠ *mean*   5 strong   ≠ *weak*

3 kind   ≠ *unkind*   6 optimistic ≠ *pessimistic*

44.4
12 marks

Fill the gaps in the text with suitable words from the box. (There are more words in the box than you need.)

sense	punctual	confident	trust	initiative	miserable
timid	sensible	sensitive	shy	cheerful	reserved

I spent the weekend camping with friends but it wasn't very successful. Sally is not very (1) *punctual* and we had to wait an hour for her to turn up. Apparently she had a problem with the train, but didn't have the common (2) *sense* to ring me on my mobile and warn me she would be late. Then, when she finally arrived, she had a friend with her, called Jill. She was quite nice, but so (3) *shy* that she didn't really speak to anyone for the first day. She'd got a bit more self- (4) *confident* by the end of the weekend. However, she didn't seem to have much (5) *initiative*: we were only 400 metres from a farm but Jill said she couldn't make tea because we had no water! Bill got angry at that, for no real reason, and poor Jill almost started crying. Bill's problem was that he never really wanted to go camping in the first place, so he was pretty (6) *miserable* most of the time.

45 Human feelings and actions

45.1 Match the words in the box with the definitions below.

5 marks

| jealous | upset | proud | frightened | embarrassed |

2 1 sad and angry because something unpleasant has happened
3P 2 feeling very satisfied when you (or someone close to you) has done something very well
4 3 afraid
em4 uncomfortable and often ashamed because you have done something wrong or stupid in a social situation
) 5 angry and unhappy because someone has something you want, or because someone you like or love is showing interest in another person

45.2 Complete the sentences using the correct form of the word on the right.

8 marks

1 Do you believe everyone has a right to ....*happiness*.... ?   HAPPY
2 It was a terribly ....*embarrasing*.... experience.   EMBARRASS
3 I think his ....*pride*.... was hurt when she left him.   PROUD
4 Her ....*jealousy*.... was the cause of most of their arguments.   JEALOUS
5 I don't know why he felt such ....*angry*.... .   ANGRY
6 They were all moved by the ....*sadness*.... of the occasion.   SAD
7 I was so ....*embarrased*.... when it happened.   EMBARRASS
8 I don't know why it caused so much ....*embarrassment*....   EMBARRASS

45.3 Complete the sentences below with a suitable word, <u>without</u> using *speak*, *look* or *walk*.

6 marks

1 She ....*whispered*.... in his ear so no-one would hear.
2 Please don't ....*shout*.... at me in that angry voice.
3 The soldiers had to ....*march*.... 20 miles back to their camp.
4 He ....*glanced*.... at his watch and realised it was time to go.
5 They had nothing to do so they went for a ....*stroll*.... through the woods.
6 She felt very uncomfortable because the two men sitting opposite were
....*staring*.... at her.

45.4 Match the verbs on the left with the words and phrases on the right.

6 marks

e 1 clap   a on the door   ....
c 2 point   b goodbye   ....
f 3 punch   c your finger at someone ....
a 4 knock   d the button   ....
b 5 wave   e your hands   ....
d 6 press   f someone on the arm   ....

45.5 Some of the words tested on this page are used with particular prepositions. Cover the rest of this page and then complete these sentences with the correct preposition.

5 marks

1 He's very jealous ....*of*.... his brother.
2 They knocked ....*at*.... the door but no-one answered.
3 You shouldn't point .... people.
4 I'm proud ....*of*.... my country.
5 She glanced ....*at*.... the others to see if they had noticed.

Test your English Vocabulary in Use (pre-intermediate and intermediate)

46 Family and friends

46.1

11 marks

Read the short text, then complete the sentences below.

This is James Thomas Brown; he has no brothers
and sisters. His parents died when he was 20 and
they left him their house. He married Julia and they
had two children, but unfortunately his wife died
two years ago. Recently he has fallen in love with
Amy who he has known since they were young. She
is the sister of a very good friend of his called Mike,
who he likes and trusts.

1 James is his ....._first_..... name.
2 James Thomas Brown is his ....._full_..... name.
3 Thomas is his ....._middle_..... name.
4 Brown is his ....._surname_..... .
5 He has no brothers and sisters so he is an ....._only_..... child.
6 At the age of 20, James ....._inherited_..... his parents' house.
7 His wife, Julia, died so he is a ....._widower_..... .
8 The two children and he form a ....._single–parent_..... family.
9 Amy is his present ....._girlfriend_..... .
10 Mike is a very ....._close_..... friend.
11 If James marries Amy, she will become the children's ....._step_..... -mother.

46.2

13 marks

Complete the definitions with a suitable word.

1 My father's brothers are my ....._uncle_..... .
2 My father's sisters are my ....._aunt_..... .
3 My sister's husband is my ....._brother–in-law_..... .
4 My brother's wife is my ....._sister–in-law_..... .
5 My wife's mother is my ....._mother–in-law_..... .
6 My aunt and uncle's children are my ....._cousins_..... .
7 My parents' parents are my ....._grandparents_..... .
8 My brother's daughters are my ....._nieces_..... .
9 My sister's sons are my ....._nephews_..... .
10 My father's first wife, who is still alive, is his ....._ex-wife_..... .
11 My oldest brother died, so his wife is a ....._widow_..... .
12 My mother remarried last year: her new husband is my ....._step–father_..... .
13 All of these people are members of my family, so they are my ....._relative_..... .

46.3

6 marks

Match the words on the left with the definitions on the right.

1 colleague   4 a the one friend you feel closest to
2 partner   3 b a man that a woman used to go out with
3 ex-boyfriend   6 c one of the parents of your husband or wife
4 best friend   5 d someone you have known well for a long time
5 old friend   1 e someone you work with
6 father-in-law   f this word is used for the person that someone loves and lives with,
        2 without indicating if they are married

Your score

/30

47 Ages and stages

47.1 Complete this story of Marianne's life using a suitable verb (in the correct tense) in each gap.

12 marks

Marianne was (1) _born_ in a hospital just five minutes from the house where her parents lived, and she (2) _grew_ up in the same house. When she was fifteen she (3) _met_ Paul at a disco. He became her first real boyfriend and she (4) _went out_ with him for over three years, but unfortunately they (5) _split up_ when Marianne (6) _went_ to university. She had lots of boyfriends in her first year at university, then she (7) _met_ Alex. They (8) _fell_ in love and (9) _got_ married the year after Marianne graduated. They both went abroad to work for a few years but returned when they decided to start a family. And by a happy coincidence, Marianne (10) _had_ their first baby, a boy, in the same hospital where she was (11) _born_ . Now, five years later, she is (12) _expecting_ a second child.

47.2 What word or phrase could describe the people at these different ages?

10 marks

Example: 6 months old = _a baby_

1 1–2 years old   = a _toddler_
2 2–12 years old   = a _kid / child_
3 about 13–17   = a(n) _teenager_
4 18+   = an _adult_
5 22   = in your _earlier_   _twenties_
6 35   = in your _mid thirties_
7 48   = in your _late_   _forties_

47.3 Complete these dialogues with a word or phrase. Don't repeat the word in italics.

8 marks

Example: A: She was lovely at *six months old*.
           B: Yes, she was a lovely _baby_ .

1 A: Were you happy *as a child*?
   B: Yes, I had a very happy _childhood_ .
2 A: It's a terrible time *when you're 14 or 15*, don't you think?
   B: Yes, I do. I think life is very difficult during _your teens_ .
3 A: I'm sure you had *arguments* with your parents then.
   B: Oh yes, we had hundreds of _rows_ .
4 A: Did your parents enjoy their *40s and 50s*?
   B: Yes, I think people are more relaxed in _middle age_ .
5 A: Do you think you'll be bored *when you finally stop work*?
   B: No, I shall enjoy my _retirement_ .
6 A: Life can be lonely for some *elderly* people.
   B: Yes, things are tough for some people in _old age_ .
7 A: My parents have been *married for 28 years*.
   B: Yes, and it has been a very happy _marriage_ , hasn't it?
8 A: Did you know Carol was *expecting a baby*?
   B: No, I didn't know she was _pregnant_ .

Your score
/30

48 Daily routines

48.1
8 marks

Correct the mistakes in these sentences.

1 I live by my own.
2 I usually go to the bed about midnight.
3 Most nights I sleep very quickly.
4 In the morning I have a shower and shave me.
5 I usually have the breakfast about 7.30.
6 After breakfast I clean the teeth.
7 I arrive to work about 8.30.
8 After work I sometimes make the shopping.

48.2
9 marks

Complete the sentences.

1 If I'm very tired in the evening I often have dinner and then I _fall_ asleep on the sofa.

2 I don't want the cats to go hungry, so I always _feed_ them and give them some water before I go to work.

3 If I'm going to work at the office in the morning, I usually _leave_ home about 8 am.

4 At work I have coffee around 11 am, and then I usually take a lunch _break_ between 12.30 and 1.00, but it's never more than half an hour.

5 If I go out to a disco in the evening and have a _late_ night, I have to set my alarm clock, otherwise I never _wake up_ in the morning.

6 I don't go out most evenings. Quite often I _stay in_ and watch TV.

7 I usually have a _lie in_ on Sunday mornings as I don't have to get up early and go to work.

8 I _play_ cards every Monday evening with my friends, but not for money.

48.3
6 marks

What words are being defined here?

1 to sleep too long   to _oversleep_
2 a short sleep   a _nap_
3 a small amount of food between meals   a _snack_
4 an informal word for a conversation   a _chat_
5 to wash the dishes   to do the _washing-up_
6 a person who cleans for you   a _cleaner_

48.4
7 marks

Find the best ending on the right for each verb on the left. Use each verb once only.

1 lie	3 a	the housework	....
2 get up	5 b	to bed	....
3 do	7 c	my own breakfast	....
4 go out	6 d	a rest	....
5 go	4 e	with friends	....
6 have	1 f	in bed	....
7 make	2 g	and have breakfast	....

Your score

/ 30

49 Homes and buildings

49.1 Label the drawings.

13 marks

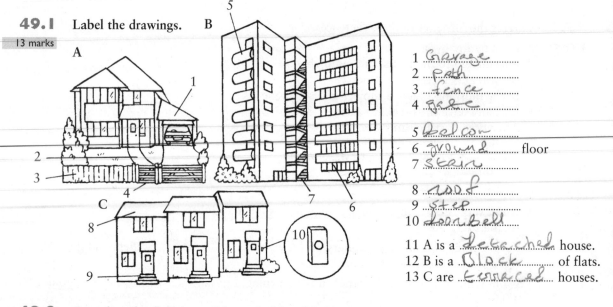

1 *Garage*
2 *path*
3 *fence*
4 *gate*
5 *Balcon*
6 *ground* floor
7 *stair*
8 *roof*
9 *step*
10 *doorbell*
11 A is a *detached* house.
12 B is a *Block* of flats.
13 C are *terraced* houses.

49.2 Complete the dialogues with a suitable adjective.

4 marks

1 A: It's cold on that side of the room because the window doesn't shut very well.
  B: Yes, if you sit over there it's very *draughty* .
2 A: Did you go and see that flat in Portland Road, then?
  B: Yes, it wasn't bad, but the living room was absolutely *narrow* ; you couldn't even put a sofa in there.
3 A: I thought you said your flat was very noisy.
  B: No, not at all in fact, it's very *quite* .
4 A: Your office is fantastic – it's absolutely *huge* !
  B: Yes, it is big, isn't it!

49.3 Rewrite the sentences using the word on the right. Start with the words you are given. The meaning must stay the same.

8 marks

1 This house is owned by a famous artist.
  This house *belongs to a famous artist.* BELONG
2 You can see the forest from the top room.
  The top room *has view of the forest.* VIEW
3 It's easy to keep the house warm.
  It's easy *to heat the house* HEAT
4 The state of the house is terrible.
  The house *is in terrible condition.* CONDITION

49.4 Are these sentences true or false?

5 marks

1 A semi-detached house is a house that stands alone and is not joined to any other house. ✗
2 Rent is the money you pay every week or month to the owner of the flat where you live. ✓
3 The person that you buy a flat from is called the landlord. ✗
4 A mortgage is the money you borrow from a bank to buy a house or flat. ✓
5 A lift is something that carries people up and down inside buildings. ✓

Your score
/30

50 Around the home I

50.1 Complete the names of these rooms in a house.

6 marks

1 The _Sitting_ room (also called the _living_) is where people watch TV.
2 The _dinning_ room is where people eat meals.
3 The _kichen_ is where people cook.
4 The _bathroom_ is where people wash or have a bath.
5 The _spare_ room is for occasional guests, and often for storing things.

50.2 Label the objects in the picture.

8 marks

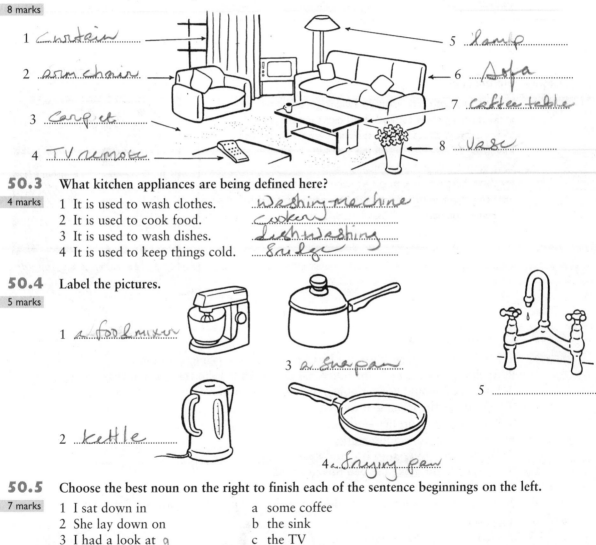

1 _curtain_
2 _arm chair_
3 _carpet_
4 _TV remote_

5 _lamp_
6 _sofa_
7 _coffee table_
8 _vase_

50.3 What kitchen appliances are being defined here?

4 marks

1 It is used to wash clothes.   _washing machine_
2 It is used to cook food.   _cooker_
3 It is used to wash dishes.   _dishwashing_
4 It is used to keep things cold.   _fridge_

50.4 Label the pictures.

5 marks

1 _a food mixer_

3 _a saucepan_

5 ....

2 _kettle_

4 _a frying pan_

50.5 Choose the best noun on the right to finish each of the sentence beginnings on the left.

7 marks

1 I sat down in   a some coffee
2 She lay down on   b the sink
3 I had a look at _g_   c the TV
4 I made _g_   d an armchair
5 He turned on _c_   e the sofa
6 I put the pans in   f a stool
7 He sat on   g the paper

51 Around the home 2

51.1
9 marks

Here are some things you find in the bedroom and bathroom, but the letters are jumbled. Put the correct words in the columns below.

malp	wehrso	ayspmaj	woltes	iltote
bredwaor	vutde	habt	lopsliw	

Bedroom
Lamp
~~durée~~
Pyjamas
Wardrobe
Pillows

Bathroom
Shower
towels
bath

51.2
6 marks

Fill the gaps.

I went to a great party last night. I didn't get home till three in the morning. I was so tired, that I didn't put my clothes away – I just ⁽¹⁾ left them all over the floor. And I forgot to ⁽²⁾ turn off the light. I ⁽³⁾ went to sleep with it on! Luckily I remembered to ⁽⁴⁾ set my alarm, because I had to get up early this morning. Ugh! I've just seen myself in the ⁽⁵⁾ mirror and I look awful! Maybe I'll look better if I ⁽⁶⁾ have a wash.

51.3
9 marks

Circle the correct answer.

1 My jeans were dirty/clean, so I had to do some washing/washing-up.
2 At the end of the meal the others sat down while I did the washing/washing-up.
3 I decided I would hoover/polish the dining room table after breakfast.
4 I did/made the ironing at the weekend.
5 She put on/put off her clothes.
6 I hate housework/houseworks.
7 Quick, get into/go into bed and keep very quiet.
8 I forgot to do/make my bed this morning.

51.4
6 marks

Match the words on the left with the words on the right to form six nouns.

1 chest   3 a clock
2 wash   6 b work
3 alarm   5 c rail
4 bedside   2 d basin
5 towel   e e of drawers
6 house   4 f table

Your score
/30

52 Everyday problems

52.1

6 marks

Fill the gaps in these dialogues. Write one word in each gap.

1 A: What's the matter?
 B: I don't know. I turned your personal stereo on but it's not ~~w o/ batteries~~
 A: Well, I've been using it a lot recently, so it probably needs new ~~batteries~~ .
 B: Yes, probably.
2 A: Is that public phone still ...... out ...... of ...... order ...... ?
 B: Yes, it seems so. It's been like that for over a week now.
3 A: You can't use the washing machine.
 B: Why not?
 A: There's something ...... wrong ...... with ...... it. The engineer is coming tomorrow.

52.2

8 marks

Look at the pictures and complete the texts.

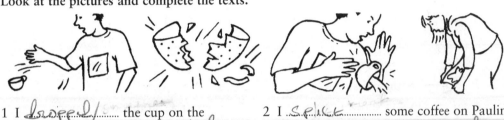

1 I ~~dropped~~ the cup on the floor and I'm afraid it ~~smashed~~ .

2 I ~~spilt~~ some coffee on Pauline's skirt, and there's a horrible ~~mark~~ on it. She won't be able to remove it.

52.3

10 marks

Complete the text using words from the box. Remember to put the verbs in the correct form. There are more words in the box than you need.

burn	humour	trip over	fall	mood	run	damage
finish	recognise	realise	leave	run out of	function	crash
work	remark	break	become	forget	get	ruin

My husband Pete wasn't in a very good (1) ~~mood~~ when I left for work this morning. He got up and discovered that we had (2) ~~run out of~~ coffee, so he had to have tea, which he hates. Then he had to iron a shirt before he could go to work. While he was doing that, the phone rang. He ran to answer it and, of course, forgot about the iron. When he came back he had (3) ~~burnt~~ a big hole in one sleeve of his shirt and it was completely (4) ~~ruined~~ ; he'll have to buy a new one. But things (5) ~~got~~ even worse: he set off for work, and (6) ~~left~~ his briefcase behind with all his notes for a very important business meeting.
Mind you, I didn't have a great start either: I (7) ~~tripped over~~ the children's toys and (8) ~~fell~~ down the stairs. Fortunately I didn't really hurt myself, but when I got to my feet I (9) ~~realised~~ I had also knocked a lamp over, and now it's not (10) ~~working~~ .

52.4

6 marks

Circle the correct word.

1 I'm afraid I've forgotten / (left) my notes at home.
2 I think he must have lost / (missed) the train – he should be here by now.
3 She got out / (got off) the bus and walked to school.
4 Have you (forgotten) / left your homework?
5 I've asked lots of people if they have seen the bag I (lost) / missed.
6 This new watch of mine isn't working (properly) / fine.

53 Money

53.1 Put these words in order from (1) the least expensive to (5) the most expensive.

5 marks

quite expensive ☐3☐   reasonable ☐2☐

incredibly expensive ☐5☐   cheap ☐1☐   very expensive ☐4☐

53.2 Complete the table below.

6 marks

Verb	Past tense	Past participle
do	did	done
buy	bought	"
spend	spent	"
lend	lent	
sell	sell	
pay	paid	
cost	cost	"

53.3 Complete these dialogues.

12 marks

1 A: Do you know, I've __spent__ over £200 this week on food.
   B: That's a lot. Have you got a big family?
2 A: Oh no, I've left my money at home. Could you __lend/pay__ me £5? I promise I'll __borrow__ you back tomorrow.
   B: No, I can't. I had to __paid__ some money myself from my sister.
3 A: Was the holiday expensive?
   B: No, not really. We __paid__ £50 a night for the hotel, and the flight __cost__ us about £150.
4 A: Are you going away again this year?
   B: No, I can't __afford__ another holiday, I'm afraid.
5 A: You're very careful with your money these days.
   B: Yes, I'm __saving__ up for a new mountain bike.
6 A: Do you know how much those earrings are __worth__ ?
   B: Yes, I had them valued at £300.
7 A: Was it expensive to get your watch repaired?
   B: Yes, they __charged__ me £80 to repair the watch and £20 for a new strap.
8 A: I wouldn't __lend__ Paul any money. He __borrow__ £50 from me last month. He said he would give it back, but he hasn't returned any of it.

53.4 Complete these definitions using words from the box.

7 marks

| sterling | coins | standard | waste | cost | currency | notes |

1 The amount that people pay for things in a country is called the __cost__ of living.
2 The level of money and comfort people have is called their __standard__ of living.
3 The type of money used in a country is called the __currency__. In the USA it is the dollar; in Britain it is called __sterling__.
4 Money can be paper money called __notes__ or pieces of metal called __coins__.
5 To __waste__ money means to use money badly.

Your score

/30

54.1 Match the sentence halves, using each half once only.

8 marks

1 If someone feels sick   *7* a they may have a cold.
2 If someone's got flu   *4* b they want to go to the toilet.
3 If someone has a heart attack *5* c they keep sneezing.
4 If someone's got diarrhoea   *1* d they want to vomit.
5 If someone's got hay fever   *8* e they feel very hot.
6 If someone's got a hangover   *2* f their muscles ache.
7 If someone is blowing their nose a lot *3* g they need a doctor immediately.
8 If someone's got a temperature *6* h they drank too much beer last night.

54.2 Write a sentence describing each person's ache or pain. Begin: *He/she's got (a/an)* …

7 marks

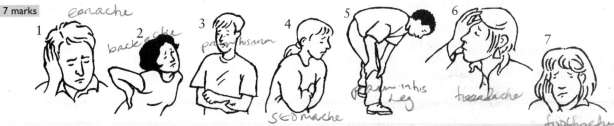

earache
backache
pain in his arm
stomache
Pain in his leg
toothache
toothache

54.3 Complete the dialogues with a word from the box.

9 marks

fillings	nose	painful	prescription	painless
sore	fever	hurt	injection	

A: Oh, dear, my eyes are really (1) ...sore... .
B: Are they?
A: Yes, and I've got a runny (2) ...nose... too.
B: Hmm, I can see that. Do you suffer from hay (3) ...fever... ?
A: Not usually, no. Maybe I should go and see the doctor.
B: Yes, then she can give you a (4) ...prescription... for the chemist's.

C: Did I tell you I fell and (5) ...hurt... my knee?
D: No – did you go and see the doctor?
C: No, I didn't, but maybe I should, because it still feels very (6) ...painfull... .

E: Have you been to the dentist's yet?
F: Yes, I went yesterday. I had to have two (7) ...fillings... in my back teeth.
E: Did he give you an (8) ...injection... ?
F: Yes, he did. I don't like needles, but it was (9) ...painless... , so I was very relieved.

54.4 Correct the mistakes. There is one in each sentence.

6 marks

1 She's in bed because she's got a flu and she feels sick.
2 It's horrible when you have a cold and keep blowing the nose.
3 My back is very pain because I was carrying a heavy suitcase yesterday.
4 His finger injured when he shut it in the door.
5 He's got a sore cough and a throat.
6 I hurt me when I ran into the tree.
myself

55 Health: injuries

55.1
5 marks

Label the pictures with words from the box below.

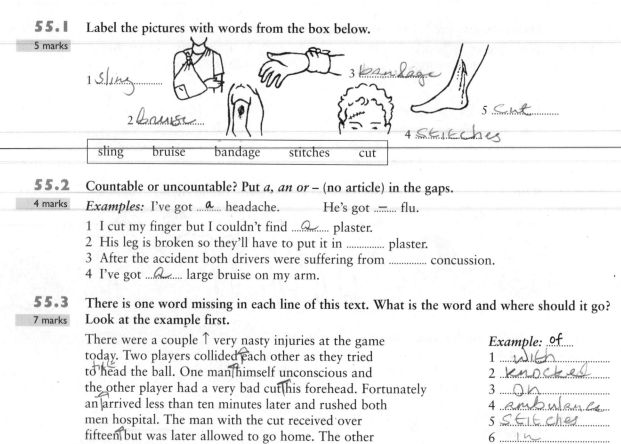

1 *sling*
2 *bruise*
3 *bandage*
5 *cut*
4 *stitches*

| sling | bruise | bandage | stitches | cut |

55.2
4 marks

Countable or uncountable? Put *a, an* or – (no article) in the gaps.

Examples: I've got ...*a*... headache.   He's got ...*–*... flu.

1 I cut my finger but I couldn't find ...*a*... plaster.
2 His leg is broken so they'll have to put it in .... plaster.
3 After the accident both drivers were suffering from .... concussion.
4 I've got ...*a*... large bruise on my arm.

55.3
7 marks

There is one word missing in each line of this text. What is the word and where should it go? Look at the example first.

There were a couple ↑ very nasty injuries at the game
today. Two players collided each other as they tried
to head the ball. One man himself unconscious and
the other player had a very bad cut his forehead. Fortunately
an arrived less than ten minutes later and rushed both
men hospital. The man with the cut received over
fifteen but was later allowed to go home. The other
man was kept hospital overnight.

Example: of
1 *with*
2 *knocked*
3 *on*
4 *ambulance*
5 *stitches*
6 *in*
7 *in*

55.4
8 marks

Complete the sentences.

1 The trouble started outside the disco when two groups of youths got into a ...*fight*... .
   One of them was ...*stabbed*... in the back with a knife but the injury was not serious.
2 The thief had a gun and the shopkeeper was ...*shot*... in the leg.
3 A: I ...*burnt*... my hand lighting that cigarette.
   B: Oh, I should think that hurts.
   A: Yes, it's very ...*painfull*...
4 I dropped a box on my foot. My toes are so ...*swollen*... that I can't get my shoes on.
5 She twisted her ...*ankle*... running for the bus.
6 I cut my finger and it won't stop ...*bleeding*... .

55.5
6 marks

Match the words on the left with the words on the right to form six phrases.

1 black   5 a wound   ....
2 swollen   6 b treatment   ....
3 broken   2 c ankle   ....
4 blood   3 d ribs   ....
5 bullet   1 e eye   ....
6 hospital   4 f test   ....

Test your English Vocabulary in Use (pre-intermediate and intermediate)

56.1 Label what the people are wearing in the pictures.

16 marks

1 Shirt
2 Shirt
3 tie
4 belt
9 skirt

5 earring
6 necklace
14
7 blouse
8 Jacket
10 knee
11 boots
16 Jeans

12 hat
13 skirt
15 gloves

56.2 Correct the mistakes in these sentences.

6 marks

Example: When I got home last night, I got <u>dressed</u> and went straight to bed.
undressed

1 I put off my clothes and got into the shower. *took*
2 I got dress, left the house and drove to the office. *buy enough*
3 I tried the jacket on but it wasn't enough big, so I asked for a smaller size.
4 The trousers were too much long so I didn't buy them.
5 He took his jacket off and carefully hung it down in the wardrobe.
6 The sleeves weren't long enough, so the jacket didn't size me very well. *didn't fit me*

56.3 Complete the crossword. When you have finished, the words in the tinted box will spell another word.

8 marks

1 It is the part of a shirt nearest the hands.
2 This part of a shirt or jacket goes round the neck.
3 It is where you put money in your trousers or jacket.
4 These are on the front of your shirt, jacket or coat, and you fasten them.
5 Women wear these on their legs.
6 The part of a shirt or jumper that covers your arms.
7 Oh, no, it's the wrong .... It's too small.

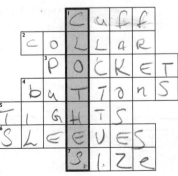

1 C U F F
2 C O L L A R
3 P O C K E T
4 b u T T o n S
5 T I G H T S
6 S L E E V E S
7 S I Z E

57 Shops and shopping

57.1

6 marks

Add two more examples to each word to form compound nouns or common phrases.

shop *keeper*　　　　*do the*　　　 shopping　　　shopping **bag**

　　 Assisant　　　　　*go*　　　　　　　　　　　　*list*

　　 Window　　　　　　　　　　　　　　　　　　　　*basket*

57.2

6 marks

Complete the sentences below with the correct 'general' word. Look at the example first.

Example: It's a very cheap place to buy ....*household goods*.... such as washing powder and other cleaning products.

1 The wardrobe was full of ....*clothes*....: dresses, jackets, trousers and skirts.
2 There were ....*toys*.... all over the children's room: teddy bears, dolls and Lego.
3 I need to buy some ....*stationary*....: a pen, writing paper and envelopes.
4 There was too much ....*furniture*.... in the room: tables, chairs, armchairs everywhere.
5 ....*Department store*.... such as TVs, stereos and washing machines are very cheap in this country.
6 She was wearing beautiful ....*jewellary*....: a lovely gold necklace and earrings.

57.3

8 marks

What are the names of these shops?

1 the place where you can buy furniture, toys, televisions, watches, etc. *Depare*
2 the place where you can buy any type of food or household goods *Supermarke*
3 the place where you can just buy meat *butcher*
4 the place where you can just buy fruit and vegetables *gr*
5 the place where you can buy fashionable clothes *boneique*
6 the place where you can buy medicine *Chemist*
7 the place where you can buy newspapers and cigarettes
8 the place where you can buy shoes *Shoe*

57.4

10 marks

Complete these shopping dialogues. You will need one or two words for each gap.

A ASSISTANT:　Can I (1) *help* you?
　CUSTOMER:　Yes, I'm (2) *Looking for* a pair of trousers.
　ASSISTANT:　Right. What (3) *size* are you?
　CUSTOMER:　32 waist and 34 leg.

B ASSISTANT:　Are you OK there?
　CUSTOMER:　Yes, I'm just (4) *Looking*, thanks.

C ASSISTANT:　Do you need any help?
　CUSTOMER:　No, it's OK, I'm being (5) *served*, thanks.

D CUSTOMER:　Excuse me. I'd like to (6) *try on* these jeans to see if they fit.
　ASSISTANT:　Sure. The (7) *Changing room* is along there at the back of the shop.

E ASSISTANT:　Do you want this red jumper as well?
　CUSTOMER:　No, I think I'll (8) *leave* it, thanks.

F CUSTOMER:　Yes, these trousers are great and fit very well. I'll (9) *take* them.
　ASSISTANT:　Fine. Would you like to pay for them over at the (10) *Counter* ?
　CUSTOMER:　Sure.

58.1 Label the food.

15 marks

1 _Cabbage_
2 _Peppers_
3 _Carrot_
4 _Cauliflower_
5 _Potatoes_
6 _green beans_
7 _peas_

8 _Banana_
9 _Grape_
10 _Lemon_
11 _orange_
12 _pere_
13 _Apple_
14 _Strewberries_
15 _peach_

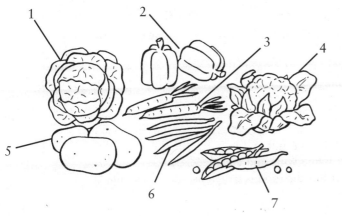

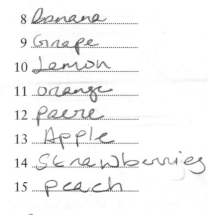

58.2 Complete these sentences with a suitable word. The first letter of the missing word is given.

8 marks

1 There are four vegetables I really hate: peppers, courgettes, m..u.sh.room... and a...aubergine....

2 We had a delicious salad of tomato, cucumber and l...Lettuce....

3 The dessert was fresh fruit: there was a large bowl of strawberries, peaches, c..herries... and p..ane apple....

4 I'm always ill if I eat certain shellfish like shrimps, o..ysters... or m..ussels...... .

5 I'm a vegetarian, so I don't eat beef, pork, lamb or v..eal.......... .

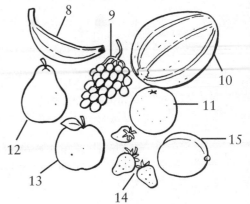

58.3 Are these sentences true or false? If they are false, correct them.

7 marks

1 Lobster is a kind of fruit. ✗ _shellfish_
2 Salad is usually a mixture of uncooked vegetables. ✓
3 A lamb is a baby sheep; lamb is also the name of the meat of that animal. ✓
4 A calf is a young pig. _D cow_
5 Salmon is a kind of shellfish. _kind of fish_

Your score

/30

6 Oil and vinegar are often used with a green salad. ✗
7 Peas, courgettes, aubergines and cucumbers are all the same colour.
 ✓ is purple

Cooking and restaurants

59.1
5 marks

Label the pictures with the different ways of cooking.

1 ~boiling~   2 ~frying~   3 ~grill~   4 ~roast~   5 ~bake~

59.2
14 marks

Fill the gaps in these sentences with the correct noun, verb or adjective.

1 You will need to put the meat in the ...~oven~... for half an hour at 200 degrees centigrade, then reduce the temperature to 180 for the rest of the cooking time.
2 When people go out for a meal in Britain, they often have three ...~course~...: a ...~starter~..., a ...~main course~..., and a dessert.
3 If you are cooking steak, you need to turn up the ...~heat~... so that your pan is really hot before you put the meat in.
4 When I pay for my meal, I usually leave 10% for the waiter if ...~service~... is not included.
5 There are basically four ways of cooking steak: ...~rare~..., medium-...~rare~..., medium, or ...~well done~.... I like my steak medium.
6 The trouble with fattening food is that it makes you ...~put on~... weight if you're not very careful.
7 Have you asked the waiter for the ...~menu~... and the wine list?
8 I'm not very keen on curry: it's too hot and ...~spicy~... for me.
9 The chicken is cooked in a white wine and cream ...~sauce~....
10 It's a very simple restaurant but the food is delicious and everything is ...~home~...-made.

59.3
6 marks

Complete Column 2 with a word that is the opposite of the word in Column 1. The first one has been done for you.

Column 1		Column 2	
strong coffee		**weak**	coffee
1 tough meat		~tender~	meat
2 fatty meat		~lean~	meat
3 sweet oranges	is/are the opposite of	~bitter~	oranges
4 tasteless food		~tasty~	food
5 cooked onions		~raw/uncooked~	onions
6 stale bread		~fresh~	bread

59.4
5 marks

Replace the underlined word(s) in these sentences with (an)other word(s) with the same meaning.

1 Do you always leave money for the waiter?   ~a tip~   ~book~   ~in advance~
2 It's a very popular restaurant, so you may need to reserve a table one or two weeks before you go there.
3 Do you want a drink before the meal? ~an aperitif~
4 Have you already paid the money for the meal?   ~bill~

Your score

/30

Town and country

60.1 Complete these definitions with a suitable word.

6 marks

1 You can borrow books or study there: _Library_
2 You can leave your car there with a lot of other cars: _Car Park._
3 A place with different kinds of shops, indoors or outdoors: _shopping centre._
4 A place where goods (washing machines, furniture, etc.) are made: _factory._
5 The areas outside the city centre where people live: _residine_
6 An area where there are company offices and banks in a town: _commercial area._

60.2 Complete the sentences using the correct form of the word on the right.

8 marks

1 Some people feel that towns are too _noisy_ for them to live in.   NOISE
2 Generally, the countryside is less _polluted_ than towns.   POLLUTE
3 Living in cities can be very _stressful_ for some people.   STRESS
4 The countryside is much less _crowded_ than towns.   CROWD
5 Some people enjoy the countryside more because it's _peaceful_.   PEACE
6 I always feel _safer_ in town than in the countryside.   SAFE
7 However, life in town is certainly more _exciting_.   EXCITE
8 Some people believe it is more _dangerous_ to live in town.   DANGER

60.3 Look at the picture, then complete the text below.

8 marks

This is a picture of a scene in the (1)c _ountryside_ . In the distance, you can see a church in the (2)v _alley_ between the two hills, and on the right-hand hill there is a small (3)w _ood_ . There is a (4)f _ootpath_ leading down from the trees back to the road, and there is a hole or space in the (5)h _____ where you can get through. If you walk along the road towards the cows, you pass a wooden (6)g _ate_ , and in the (7)f _ield_ behind that, there is a farmer driving a (8)t _ractor_ .

60.4 Match the sentence halves.

8 marks

1 There are only   8   a much better than in the countryside.
2 There is a wide range   3   b very little to do in the countryside.
3 At night there is   1   c a few shops in the countryside.
4 There are plenty of   2   d of shops in town.
5 There is a lot of   2   e things to do in town.
6 The countryside has   5   f pollution in town.
7 Living in town can be   6   g lots of open space.
8 The nightlife in the city is   7   h stressful and dangerous.

Your score
/30

On the road

61.1 Label the picture, using the words in the box.

12 marks

pedestrians	road sign	pedestrian crossing	main road
traffic jam	petrol station	roadworks	bend
traffic lights	pavement	junction	lorry

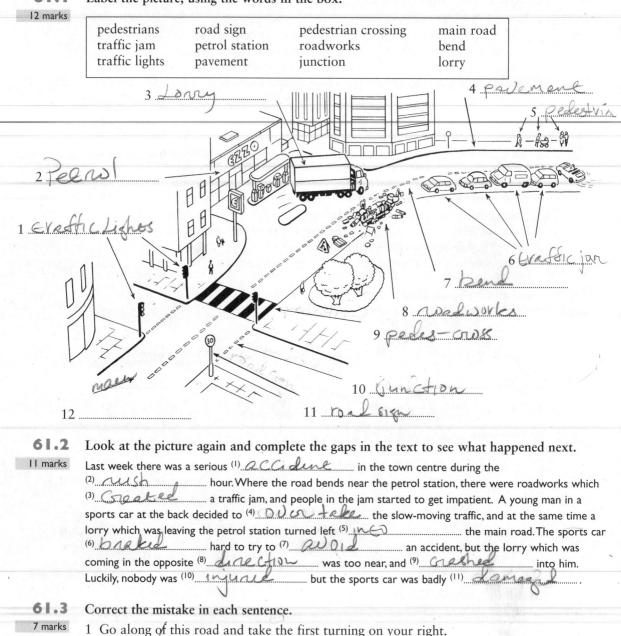

3 _Lorry_

4 _pavement_

5 _pedestrin_

2 _Petrol_

1 _Traffic Lights_

6 _traffic jam_

7 _bend_

8 _roadworks_

9 _pedes-cross_

10 _Junction_

11 _road sign_

12 _maex_

61.2 Look at the picture again and complete the gaps in the text to see what happened next.

11 marks

Last week there was a serious (1) _accident_ in the town centre during the (2) _rush_ hour. Where the road bends near the petrol station, there were roadworks which (3) _created_ a traffic jam, and people in the jam started to get impatient. A young man in a sports car at the back decided to (4) _overtake_ the slow-moving traffic, and at the same time a lorry which was leaving the petrol station turned left (5) _into_ the main road. The sports car (6) _braked_ hard to try to (7) _avoid_ an accident, but the lorry which was coming in the opposite (8) _direction_ was too near, and (9) _crashed_ into him. Luckily, nobody was (10) _injured_ but the sports car was badly (11) _damaged_.

61.3 Correct the mistake in each sentence.

7 marks

1 Go along of this road and take the first turning on your right.
2 He got on the car, fastened his seat belt and drove away.
3 Keep go down here, until you get to the bank.
4 The lorry broke in the inside lane of the motorway.
5 If you drive in the fast lane of the motorway, be careful not to break the limit of speed.
6 He overtake the bicycle on the bridge, which caused a serious accident.
7 The post office is down there – turn on the left at the traffic lights.

62.1 Label the pictures.

6 marks

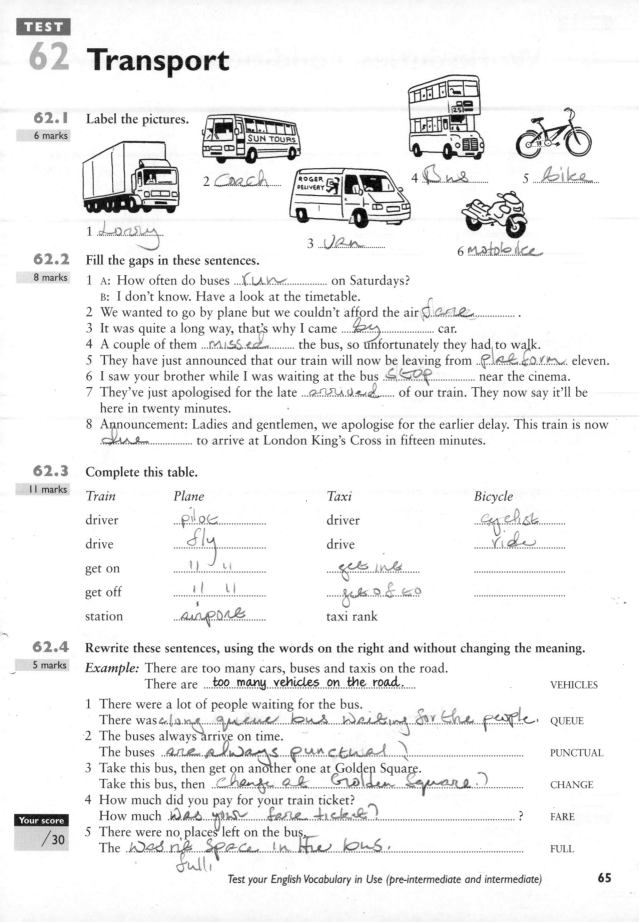

2 _Coach_

4 _Bus_

5 _bike_

1 _Lorry_

3 _Van_

6 _motorbike_

62.2 Fill the gaps in these sentences.

8 marks

1 A: How often do buses _run_ on Saturdays?
   B: I don't know. Have a look at the timetable.
2 We wanted to go by plane but we couldn't afford the air _fare_ .
3 It was quite a long way, that's why I came _by_ car.
4 A couple of them _missed_ the bus, so unfortunately they had to walk.
5 They have just announced that our train will now be leaving from _platform_ eleven.
6 I saw your brother while I was waiting at the bus _stop_ near the cinema.
7 They've just apologised for the late _arrived_ of our train. They now say it'll be here in twenty minutes.
8 Announcement: Ladies and gentlemen, we apologise for the earlier delay. This train is now _due_ to arrive at London King's Cross in fifteen minutes.

62.3 Complete this table.

11 marks

Train	Plane	Taxi	Bicycle
driver	_pilot_	driver	_cyclist_
drive	_fly_	drive	_ride_
get on	_'' ''_	_gets into_	
get off	_'' ''_	_gets off so_	
station	_airport_	taxi rank	

62.4 Rewrite these sentences, using the words on the right and without changing the meaning.

5 marks

Example: There are too many cars, buses and taxis on the road.
          There are _too many vehicles on the road._   VEHICLES

1 There were a lot of people waiting for the bus.
  There was _a long queue bus waiting for the people._   QUEUE
2 The buses always arrive on time.
  The buses _are always punctual)_   PUNCTUAL
3 Take this bus, then get on another one at Golden Square.
  Take this bus, then _change at Golden Square.)_   CHANGE
4 How much did you pay for your train ticket?
  How much _was your fare ticket?)_ ?   FARE
5 There were no places left on the bus.
  The _wasn't space in the bus._   FULL
  full

63.1 Put the words in these questions in the correct order.

4 marks

1 living do do what for you a? *What do you do for you for a living*
2 you do much how earn?
3 tax you pay do have income to?
4 much do get holiday you how?
5 overtime in you do work job have to your?
6 pay you do holiday get?
7 pay get sick you do?
8 your what involve does job?

63.2 Match the questions above with the answers below.

4 marks

a Yes, if we are very busy.
b Yes, up to six months' full salary.
c £40,000 per year.
d Yes, I pay 40% a year to the government.
e I deal with overseas clients, mainly.
f 28 days.
g I work for an international bank.
h Yes, it's included in my salary.

63.3 Replace the <u>underlined</u> words or phrases with a suitable alternative.

6 marks

1 I must leave – I have to <u>go to</u> a very important meeting.
2 My wife is <u>in charge of</u> about twenty workers in her department.
3 How long have you been <u>managing</u> this shop?
4 I quite often have to <u>work</u> overtime, but I don't mind, because I'm paid for it.
5 My job involves <u>meeting</u> clients and advising them on their financial problems.
6 Could you tell me what your <u>duties</u> are?

63.4 Match the words and phrases on the left with those on the right.

6 marks

1 to work flexi-time	a	working at different times: days one week, nights the next
2 to run a business	b	to work regular daytime hours
3 to have a nine-to-five job	c	money you earn every month/year
4 to do paperwork	d	to manage or be responsible for a company
5 to do shiftwork	e	to do routine work such as writing letters, filling in forms
6 a salary	f	to be able to start and finish work at different times each day

63.5 Correct the <u>ten</u> mistakes in these sentences. (Sentences 1 and 6 both have <u>two</u> mistakes.)

10 marks

1 I'm builder and I work to a big company in the city of London.
2 Unfortunately, I haven't got a work at the moment, but I hope to find one soon.
3 I work on a hospital in the X-ray department.
4 What your job involves, exactly?
5 I have to deal the delivery problems in my company.
6 I make a lot of paperwork, which involves fill in a lot of forms.
7 I am pay a very good salary.
8 I have to advice clients a lot in my job.

64 Jobs

64.1 **What jobs are defined here?**

8 marks

1 Someone who teaches in a university, but is not a professor.
2 Someone who plans the building of roads, bridges, machines, etc.
3 Someone who is a doctor for animals.
4 Someone who makes things with wood.
5 Someone who fits water pipes, bathrooms, etc.
6 Someone who looks after your teeth.
7 Someone who controls the financial situation of individuals and companies.
8 Someone who fits and services electrical things.

64.2 **What do the people in these jobs do? Fill the gaps with a suitable verb. The first letter has**

8 marks **been given to you.**

1 Doctors t................................. patients.
2 Lawyers a.................................. and represent people with legal problems.
3 Nurses l................................. .... patients in hospital.
4 Surgeons o................................. on people.
5 Mechanics r................................. cars.
6 Bricklayers b................................. walls.
7 Architects d................................. buildings.
8 Brokers b................................. and s................................. stocks and shares.

64.3 **Identify the jobs of these people and the organisations they work for. Look at the example.**

8 marks

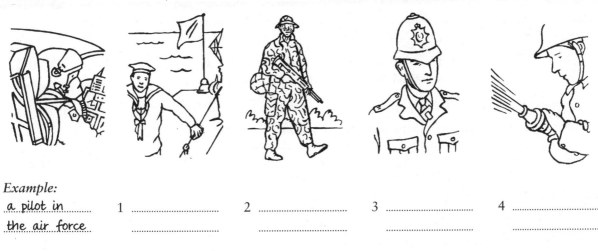

Example:
a pilot in   1 ....   2 ....   3 ....   4 ....
the air force
....

64.4 **Complete this short text with suitable words.**

6 marks   Jobs where you work with your hands and don't need any ability or training are called (1).................................
jobs. If you work with your hands but the job requires a lot of ability and training, we call it a
(2)................................. job. We refer to doctors and lawyers as professional people: doctors work in the
(3)................................. profession, lawyers work in the (4)................................. profession. The people who
defend the country, such as soldiers and sailors, are part of the (5)................................. forces. Firefighters and
ambulance drivers are part of the (6)................................. services.

65 The career ladder

65.1

Rewrite these sentences, using the words on the right in the correct form. The meaning must stay the same.

1 I did a training course last week.
Last week I .... GO
2 The boss dismissed him when he heard about the scandal.
The boss .... GIVE SOMEONE THE SACK
3 She quit her job because of the long hours.
She .... RESIGN
4 I am now in charge of both departments.
I am now .... RESPONSIBLE
5 In his job he has to travel a lot.
His job .... INVOLVE
6 I was very well paid in my last job.
I .... EARN

65.2

Decide whether the pairs of sentences have the same meaning or a different meaning.

1 a) They gave him a lot of training when he started in the job.
   b) They organised a lot of help and advice when he started the job.
2 a) She was given a pay rise at the end of the year.
   b) She was dismissed at the end of the year.
3 a) He decided it was time to take control of the sister company.
   b) He decided it was time to take over the sister company.
4 a) I've been out of work for weeks.
   b) I've been unemployed for weeks.
5 a) The company has decided to sack him.
   b) The company has decided to promote him.
6 a) She's going to leave and look for an easier job.
   b) She's going to leave and look for a fresh challenge.

65.3

Correct the mistake in each sentence.

1 I'd like to apply that job, but I don't think I'll get it.
2 He got a job like a manager in the shoe department.
3 He's going to be retire at the age of 60.
4 We are giving him a training to help him.
5 He promoted and they gave him a pay rise.
6 I'm looking for a half-time job but I'll take anything which is interesting.

65.4

Fill the gaps with a suitable word.

1 I didn't .... much money in my last job but I'm well paid now.
2 He works very hard for the company and his future .... look good.
3 I've decided to retire .... the age of 55.
4 I've got an interesting job which .... working with young people.
5 I've been unemployed for two months and I'm .... for work.
6 If I was very unhappy I would probably .... from the company and work from home.

66 In the office and in the factory

66.1 Label the drawing.

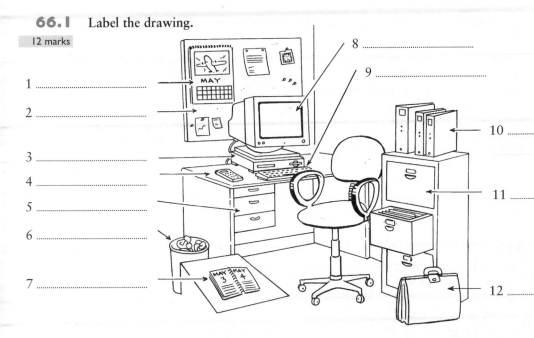

12 marks

1 ....

2 ....

3 ....

4 ....

5 ....

6 ....

7 ....

8 ....

9 ....

10 ....

11 ....

12 ....

66.2 Complete the sentences with an appropriate verb in the correct form. The first letter has been given to you.

4 marks

1 In our office everyone w.. at a computer.
2 The secretary a.. phone calls from customers and a.. meetings for her boss.
3 My job is to s.. invoices to our customers.
4 The department manager sometimes has to s.. visitors round the factory.
5 The office assistant d.. general paperwork such as f.. reports and w.. memos.

66.3 Match the words with the correct definition.

6 marks

1 the things that are made in a factory to be sold
2 where the products are manufactured in the factory
3 where the products are kept when they leave the factory
4 the people who check the products during manufacture
5 the process of making goods which is done by machines
6 the arrangement of the factory where each worker makes part of the product, then passes it to the next worker to continue

a assembly line
b warehouse
c goods
d automation
e the shop floor
f supervisors

66.4 Decide if the underlined word is correct or not. If not, correct it.

8 marks

In my company, we (1) fabricate children's toys. The parts of these toys are often very small, so the workers can find these toys very difficult to (2) assemble. When supervisors (3) control the goods, they have to make sure they meet the required safety (4) standard. It is very important when selling toys that the goods are attractively (5) packeted. The goods are sent to the warehouse where they are (6) stored until the (7) retailers order them. They are usually then (8) carried to the shops by post.

Your score

/30

67.1 **A: Match words on the left with words on the right to form six common word partnerships.**

6 marks

1 raw *e*	a cut	....
2 interest *c*	b economy	....
3 tax *a*	c rate	....
4 break *f*	d expenditure	....
5 public *d*	e materials	....
6 strong *b*	f even	....

4 marks

B: Answer these questions about Part A.

1 Which word/phrase above is not directly related to money?
2 Which word/phrase above refers to a reduction?
3 Which word/phrase above refers to money spent?
4 Which word/phrase above is usually expressed as a percentage, which may go up or down?

67.2 **Complete these sentences. You need one word only in each sentence.**

8 marks

1 Money you borrow from a bank is called a ....*loan*........ .
2 If a company expands, it is getting ....*bigger*........ .
3 Money a company earns from selling its products is the ....*turnover*........ .
4 If a company is thriving, it is doing ....*well*........ .
5 The continuous increase in the price of things is known as ....
6 When there is a period of slow business activity, we say the economy is in
   ....
7 The regular costs involved in running a company, e.g. rent, telephone, paper, etc., are
   called the ....
8 When you borrow money you have to pay .... to the bank.

67.3 **Fill the gaps in the text. The first letter of each missing word is given, and the picture should help you as well.**

12 marks

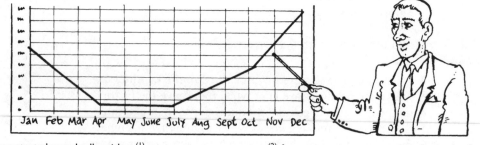

The year started very badly with a (1) s.................................... (2) f.................................... in sales in the first quarter. This was largely due to the strength of the pound and very high (3) i.................................... (4) r.................................... for the business sector. Fortunately there was an improvement in the second half of the year. Sales stopped (5) f.................................... by May, they began to (6) r.................................... (7) s.................................... during the summer and early autumn and then in November and December they (8) r.................................... (9) d.................................... and left the company feeling much more optimistic about the future. Overall perhaps it had not been a great year, but the chairman thought the company would still (10) m.................................... a reasonable (11) p.................................... on the trading for the whole year, despite the (12) l.................................... suffered in the first quarter.

Your score

/30

Sales and marketing

68.1 Complete these definitions of the four Ps in the marketing mix.

4 marks

1 p... = what a company makes or offers
2 p... = what it costs to the buyer
3 p... = ways to make it popular and well-known
4 p... = where you sell it

68.2 Fill the gaps with a suitable word.

6 marks

1 We'll need to look at the sales .... to see how many we've sold this year.
2 The company will have to carry out a lot of market .... before they start developing the next model.
3 At present the company has a 10% market ....
4 The sales .... was 12,000 units for this year, but the first half has been quite slow so I don't think they'll reach their ....
5 It's the biggest company in the industry and has been market .... for years.

68.3 Complete each of the sentences using the correct form of the word on the right.

9 marks

1 The .... is very strong in this industry.   COMPETE
2 Do they still .... goods in that factory?   PRODUCT
3 He's one of their best sales ....   REPRESENT
4 She's applied for the job as .... manager.   MARKET
5 They lost the contract to their biggest ....   COMPETE
6 It has become a very .... product.   FASHION
7 The quality is good but .... has been a problem.   DISTRIBUTE
8 They're going to try a different kind of ....   PROMOTE
9 Packaging is very important to .... nowadays.   CONSUME

68.4 Agree with each of the questions below, using words from the box.

6 marks

glamorous	up-to-date	good value
luxury	mass-produced	reliable

1 A: They produce these in large numbers, don't they?   B: Yes, they are ....
2 A: Do you think it was worth the money?   B: Yes, it was ....
3 A: Can you trust these machines?   B: Yes, they are ....
4 A: Do people still find them exciting and attractive?   B: Yes, they find them ....
5 A: Are they a modern company?   B: Yes, they are very ....
6 A: Do they only sell cars at the top of the market?   B: Yes, only .... cars.

68.5 Cross out the one word in *italics* that cannot be used in each sentence.

5 marks

1 You can *sell, launch, compete, advertise* a product.
2 A product can be high *luxury, status, quality, prestige*.
3 You can look at sales *forecasts, leaders, targets, figures*.
4 Companies find out the needs of *customers, clients, containers, consumers*.
5 You can talk about market *share, leader, research, department*.

Your score

/30

69 Hobbies

69.1

12 marks

Complete the sentences with the correct verb and noun, using the pictures to help you. Look at the example first.

Example: I've ....**played**.... the ...**guitar**.... for ten years.

1 I've ....
 since I was nine.

2 I learned to ....
 at school.

3 We often ....
 in the summer.

4 We used to ....
 in the evening.

5 Do you .... a musical .... ?

6 She .... rare old ....

69.2

6 marks

Complete the definitions.

1 You need good boots and all the right equipment for rock ....
2 Running in a park or round the streets to keep fit is called ....
3 Walking long distances in the countryside or on hills is called ....
4 A hobby is an activity you do in your .... time.
5 Very old objects and pieces of furniture are known as ....
6 Chess and Monopoly are both examples of .... games.

69.3

12 marks

Rewrite these sentences. Start with the words you are given and include the words on the right. The meaning must stay the same.

Example: She likes swimming.
 She *is keen on swimming.*.. KEEN
1 He really enjoys DIY.
 He .... MAD
2 I make all my dresses myself.
 I .... OWN
3 We stopped it because it was just too expensive as a hobby.
 We .... GIVE UP
4 She became a member of the tennis club last year.
 She .... JOIN
5 I very often go camping in the mountains.
 I .... DO
6 I started photography when I was a teenager.
 I .... TAKE UP

Your score

/30

Sport 1: games, people and places

70.1
12 marks

Label the equipment and name the sport it is used in.
Look at the example first.

Example: ..a goal used in football..

1 ....

2 ....

3 ....

4 ....

5 ....

6 ....

7 ....

8 ....

70.2
8 marks

Fill the gaps with a suitable word.

1 I love sport. In the summer I .... tennis and in the winter I ....
a lot of skiing.
2 There was a .... of 70,000 for the last game at Wembley ....
3 It wasn't a dirty game but the .... still booked five players in the second half.
4 At the end of the game about 500 .... climbed over the fence and ran onto
the .... to cheer the players off and celebrate their 2–0 victory.
5 In the final of the tennis, the problem started when the .... overruled the
linesman and gave the point to Hingis.

70.3
6 marks

Match a word from the left with a word from the right to find the names of six places where
different sports take place.

1 swimming   a pitch   ....
2 tennis   b ring   ....
3 golf   c pool   ....
4 rugby   d track   ....
5 race   e course   ....
6 boxing   f court   ....

70.4
4 marks

Complete the text using the pictures to help you.
Put the verbs in the correct form.

Zanetti (1)........................... the ball back to his goalkeeper who (2)........................... it fifty metres upfield.
Simeone won the ball and (3)........................... to Roberto Baggio. With great skill, Baggio then beat two
defenders down the right and crossed the ball for Ronaldo to (4)........................... a spectacular goal.

71 Sport 2: winning, losing and scoring

71.1 Fill the gaps with a suitable word. The sentences are about football.

6 marks

1 The papers said that the team .... well and were very unlucky to lose.
2 From the Nou Camp Stadium we understand it is one–................................. to Barcelona at the moment but we don't know who .... the goal.
3 The .... of this match will play Real Madrid in the final.
4 A: What was the final .... , do you know?
   B: It finished 1–1, which is disappointing, but probably a fair ....

71.2 Rewrite the sentences using the words on the right (in the correct form) and without changing the meaning. You must also include all the information from the first sentence.

8 marks

1 Brazil beat Spain 2–0.

.... LOSE

2 Holland beat Denmark 3–2.

.... WIN

3 The game between Peru and Italy finished 2–2.

.... DRAW

4 England are leading 1–0.

.... LATEST

71.3 Fill the gaps in the sentences below with words from the box, which are all used in a number of different sports. You will need to put the verbs into the correct form as well.

9 marks

kick	tackle	points	book	serve
penalty	league	lap	championship	

1 Beckham has just been .... for a late .... on Bergkamp. This is already his third yellow card of the season.
2 If they win, they'll improve their .... position from sixth to third.
3 We've just heard from Monza that Schumacher has moved up into second place on the twenty-third .... of the race.
4 Roberto Carlos got the goal with a wonderful free .... from just outside the England .... area.
5 Sampras is playing well enough to win the ....
6 Whitman already has eight baskets and that's worth sixteen ....
7 Hingis .... badly, but still managed to win the game.

71.4 Write down answers to these questions.

7 marks

1 What comes between the quarter final and the final?
2 What do we call this type of competition?
3 In a game of football, if the two teams finish 2–2 after ninety minutes, they may play a further 30 minutes. What is this called?
4 If the score is still 2–2 after this 30 minutes, there is a special method to find a winner. What is it called?
5 In tennis if the score reaches 6–6, they play one final game. What is this called?
6 In tennis men play a maximum of five, women play a maximum of three. What are they?
7 We do not say fifteen–zero (15–0) in tennis. What do we say?

Your score

/30

72.1

6 marks

Label the numbered parts in the picture with words from the box.

circle
stage
aisle
curtains
stalls
rows of seats

1 ....

2 ....

3 ....

4 ....

5 ....

6 ....

72.2

12 marks

Complete these sentences and dialogues. Write one word in each gap.

1 There was a .... of hundreds of actors in *Titanic* – but the .... of the film, Leonardo diCaprio and Kate Winslet, both became very famous.

2 Steven Spielberg is the famous film .... who made ET and Schindler's List.

3 A: When you see an English film in your country, do they have .... across the bottom of the screen?

   B: Sometimes. But a lot of the films are .... and have Spanish actors speaking the part in Spanish.

4 A: Have you seen Oliver Stone's *Platoon*?

   B: No. What kind of film is it?

   A: It's a .... film, set in Vietnam in the late 1960s.

5 We went to the theatre to see a .... by a new dramatist.

6 Have you seen the papers? The new Alan Parker film has got fantastic .... ; most of the .... think it is the best film he has ever made.

7 A: Have you seen Andrew Lloyd Webber's new .... ? It has some great songs.

   B: Yes, I went yesterday. The evening .... was fully booked but I managed to get two tickets for the matinee.

8 At the end of the show, the .... stood up and clapped.

72.3

6 marks

Match adjectives on the left (often used to describe films) with the best definition on the right.

1	moving	a	exciting and very interesting
2	slow	b	not serious but enjoyable
3	violent	c	producing strong emotions, often of sadness
4	good fun	d	has a big effect on our emotions
5	powerful	e	includes lots of scenes with fighting and death
6	gripping	f	boring

72.4

6 marks

What do we call the following types of film?

1 a film that makes you laugh

2 a film with cowboys

3 a film such as Dracula

4 a film about the future

5 a very exciting film, often including some kind of crime

6 the kind of film that often has Sylvester Stallone or Arnold Schwarzenegger

Your score

/30

Music, art and literature

73.1

5 marks

Circle the correct answer.

1 He is a well-known <u>composer/compositor</u>.
2 Do you like <u>classic/classical</u> music?
3 Have you seen the latest <u>exhibition/exposition</u>?
4 Do you play a <u>music/musical</u> instrument?
5 I've never heard of him. Is he a very well-known <u>sculpture/sculptor</u>?

73.2

7 marks

Label these musical instruments.

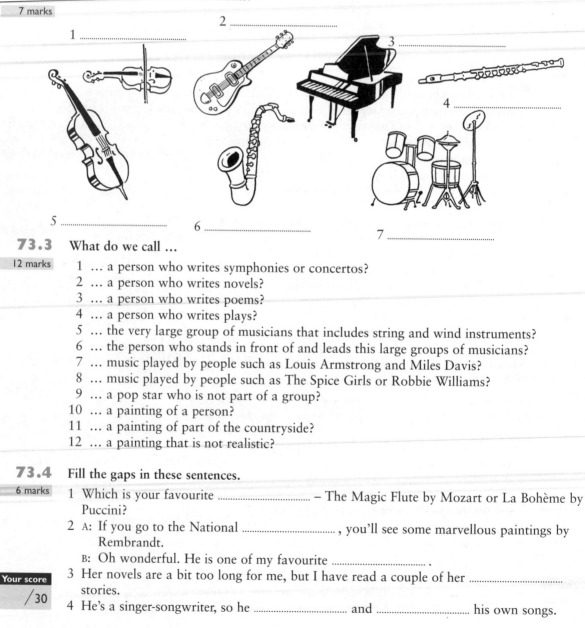

1 ....
2 ....
3 ....
4 ....
5 ....
6 ....
7 ....

73.3

12 marks

What do we call ...

1 ... a person who writes symphonies or concertos?
2 ... a person who writes novels?
3 ... a person who writes poems?
4 ... a person who writes plays?
5 ... the very large group of musicians that includes string and wind instruments?
6 ... the person who stands in front of and leads this large groups of musicians?
7 ... music played by people such as Louis Armstrong and Miles Davis?
8 ... music played by people such as The Spice Girls or Robbie Williams?
9 ... a pop star who is not part of a group?
10 ... a painting of a person?
11 ... a painting of part of the countryside?
12 ... a painting that is not realistic?

73.4

6 marks

Fill the gaps in these sentences.

1 Which is your favourite .... – The Magic Flute by Mozart or La Bohème by Puccini?
2 A: If you go to the National .... , you'll see some marvellous paintings by Rembrandt.
  B: Oh wonderful. He is one of my favourite ....
3 Her novels are a bit too long for me, but I have read a couple of her .... stories.
4 He's a singer-songwriter, so he .... and .... his own songs.

Your score

/30

74 Newspapers

74.1

4 marks

Complete this text with suitable words.

Magazines are usually weekly or monthly, but most newspapers are (1).. , in other words they are (2).. every day. Some are called (3).. , which means that they are small in size and tend to have more pictures and shorter articles. The more serious papers, larger in size, are called the (4).. or the quality press.

74.2

10 marks

Rewrite the sentences using the words on the right in the correct form. The meaning must stay the same.

1 The magazine is published every week.
The magazine ....   COME OUT

2 Five million people read that paper.
The paper ....   CIRCULATION

3 I read in one paper that they're getting married.
It ....   SAY

4 But I read in another paper that they have no plans to marry.
They have no plans to marry, ...   ACCORDING

5 There isn't much about other countries in the paper.
There isn't much ....   FOREIGN

74.3

8 marks

Replace the underlined words in the headlines below with words from the box that have the same meaning.

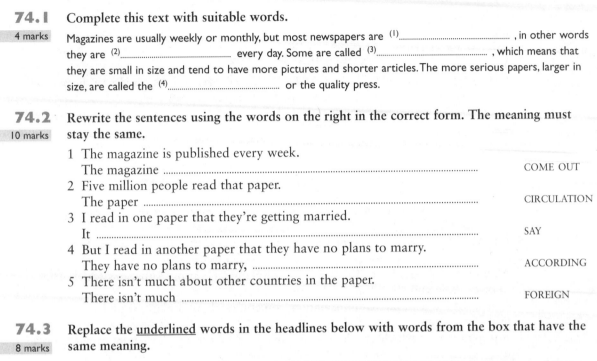

| row | bid | talks | key | cut | back | hit | quit |

1 Train service <u>badly affected</u> by storms

2 New <u>argument</u> over job scheme

3 Government to <u>reduce</u> hospital waiting lists

4 NEW <u>DISCUSSIONS</u> BEGIN NEXT WEEK

5 Transport Minister to <u>resign</u> soon

6 BANKS <u>SUPPORT</u> RESCUE PACKAGE

7 Employment is the <u>important</u> issue, says union

8 NEW <u>ATTEMPT</u> TO GO ROUND WORLD IN HOT AIR BALLON

74.4

8 marks

Fill the gaps with a suitable word.

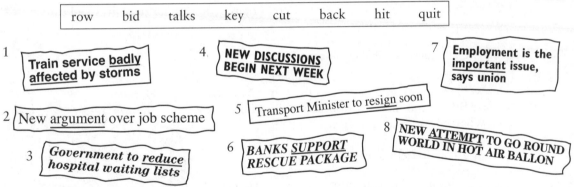

1 Did you see the .... in this morning's paper? It said NEW HOPE FOR PEACE.

2 Most of the .... are employed by the newspaper, but there are some who work .... and may write for several papers.

3 The newspaper hasn't been doing very well lately, so the owner has decided to put in a new .... to see if he can turn things round and improve sales.

4 The film .... of The Times gave his new film a really good .... in yesterday's paper.

5 Where is the weather .... in this newspaper?

6 There was a funny .... in the paper today: a picture of the Prime Minister with two heads, and one head is saying to the other, 'Yes, I completely agree with you.'

75 Television

75.1 Complete the sentences with a word from the box.

4 marks

dish	terrestrial	licence	cable

In Britain you have to have a TV (1).. and the money from it pays for the BBC. BBC 1 and BBC 2 are (2).. channels, but if you have a satellite (3).. , you can get satellite TV like Sky. Some people prefer to have (4).. TV to satellite.

75.2 Complete the definitions with a suitable word. The first letter has been given.

8 marks

1 A TV advertisement shown between programmes: a c.. .
2 A number of programmes about the same characters which makes people laugh: a
   c.. s.. .
3 A programme which is on TV several times a week and follows the lives of a group of
   characters: a s.. o.. .
4 A programme about a social or political situation which is in the news at the moment: a
   c.. a.. programme.
5 A number of programmes about a group of people in various situations which is intended
   to be exciting and interesting: a d.. s.. .
6 A programme with factual information, sometimes about a place, wildlife, a social
   problem, etc: a d.. .
7 A programme in which people have to answer questions or play games to win a prize: a
   q.. show.
8 A programme where a presenter talks to famous people about their lives and careers: a
   c.. show.

75.3 Complete the questions in the dialogue below.

8 marks

1 A: What ...do you do... tonight?
   B: Well, there's an interview with the Prime Minister
      on BBC 1 and there's a Robert de Niro film on ITV.
2 A: What .... the
      film .... ?
   B: At 10.30 – after the news.
3 A: How long .... ?
   B: About two hours, I think. Oh, I forgot! There's
      football on Channel 5 at 7.00 – it's Manchester
      United versus Barcelona.
4 A: Is .... ?
   B: No, I think it's just the recorded highlights – the match is in the afternoon.

75.4 Correct the mistake in each sentence.

10 marks

1 If your television isn't working, perhaps you have forgotten to plug it.
2 Oh, dear, this is such a boring film – look, the news is about to start on the other channel.
   Could you turn down?
3 Turn the TV up, will you – the children are trying to go to sleep.
4 Don't turn the TV on – I'm watching it.
5 The baby loves the TV. She's always trying to switch it down.

76.1

8 marks

Correct the mistakes in these telephone conversations. There are 3 mistakes in the first and 5 in the second.

1 A: Hello.
  B: Are you Susan?
  A: Yes.
  B: Oh hi. I am Maria.
  A: Hello, Maria. How are you?
  B: Thank you. And you?

2 A: Hello?
  B: Hello. Is it Mr Fantini?
  A: Yes, I am speaking.
  B: Oh good morning. Here is Pierre Kaufmann.
    I tried to phone earlier, but the line was occupied.
  A: Yes. I did a lot of calls this morning.

76.2

10 marks

Fill the gaps in these sentences with the correct word.

1 When I got home last night there were four messages on my ....
2 You can put the information in the post if you like, but it would be much quicker if you sent it by .... I'll give you the number.
3 I tried to .... through to you from a public phone .... but the first one was out of order, and the second one I tried only took phone .... , and I haven't got one.
4 If I'm not in the office, you can always reach me on my ....
5 I tried to ring Mary but she was already .... the phone to her sister.
6 If you don't know the number, you can find out from Directory ....
7 A: Did you phone your parents?
  B: Yes, but I had to make a .... charge call as I didn't have any money.
8 I had trouble getting through; in the end I had to go through the ....

76.3

12 marks

Complete the phrases in these telephone conversations.

1 A: Hello?
  B: Oh could I speak to Alex?
  A: Sorry, there's no Alex living here. I think you've got ....
2 A: Hello?
  B: Hello. Could I speak to Mrs Peterson, please?
  A: I'm afraid .... at the moment, and she won't .... until much later this afternoon. Would you like to .... ?
  B: Yes, could you tell her that Sandra rang, and that I'll .... a ring this evening at home.
3 A: Good morning. The Sheraton Hotel. How may I help you?
  B: Yes, I'd like to speak to the manager.
  A: Who's calling, please?
  B: My name is Errington – James Errington.
  A: Right, Mr Errington, if you could hold the line, I'll see if he's busy. ... Uh Mr Ratcliffe can speak to you now Mr Errington. I'll just .... through.

Your score

/30

77 Computers

77.1 Label the items in the picture.

7 marks

1 .....Monitor......

2 .....Screen......

3 .....printer......

4 .....keyboard......

5 .....c/d......

6 .....flopy......

7 .....mouse......

77.2 Match the verbs on the left with an appropriate word on the right. Use each word once only.

5 marks

1 to operate b	a a new document	....
2 to click e	b a computer	....
3 to open a	c data	....
4 to save c	d a back-up copy	....
5 to make d	e on an icon	....

77.3 Complete the sentences with a word from the box.

9 marks

virus	memory	save	print	laptop	cut	crash	copy	paste

1 If you click on .... , the computer will store the data for you.

2 If you click on .... , you will have two versions of something.

3 If you click on .... , the computer will take something out.

4 If you click on .... , it will put in something you wanted to move.

5 If you click on .... , you can get a paper copy.

6 If the computer has a .... because there is a software problem, it could

....

7 If your computer is very slow, it may need more ....

8 If you want to work on a plane or train, you need to use a .... computer.

77.4 Are these sentences true or false? If they are false, change them to make them true.

9 marks

1 Many business people use word processing to arrange numbers and financial information.

2 A graphics program helps you to produce symbols and pictures.

3 People who are computer-literate find computers hard to use.

4 You can send e-mail via the Internet.

5 Hardware is the program you need to work the machine.

6 If your machine is user-friendly, it is easy for a beginner to use.

7 A database lets you look at and change around a lot of information quickly.

8 It's easy to take the hard disk out of the computer.

9 If your computer has a bug, there is a problem with the software.

Your score

/30

78 Education: school

78.1
8 marks

Complete this description of a typical school education in many parts of Britain.

Age

3 Some children go to .... school.

5 Everyone starts .... school.

11 Children go on to .... school. Some of these are called grammar schools, others are called .... i.e. with mixed ability.

16 By law, children can .... school at this age and .... a job, but many .... at school for two more years.

18 If they pass their exams, many .... to university.

78.2
6 marks

True or false? If the sentence is false, change it to make it true, using the space below.

1 In England public schools are the same as state schools.

....

2 Children at school are called 'pupils'.

....

3 In British schools PE is short for 'practical education'.

....

4 In Britain, the academic year is usually divided into two terms.

....

5 The working day is divided into lessons, with morning and afternoon breaks.

....

6 The plan for each day's work is called the school schedule.

....

78.3
8 marks

Correct the mistake in each sentence.

1 I'd like to go to the university to study medicine.
2 Economics are very difficult to understand.
3 Physic is not a popular subject.
4 I'm not interested in politic.
5 She was tired after her lesson so she went to the bed.
6 How many subjects did you make at school?
7 She went out of school when she was sixteen.
8 I went to college with eighteen years.

78.4
8 marks

Complete the names of eight school subjects from the letters you are given.

1 Ge.ography
2 Hi.story
3 Sc.ience
4 Ma.ths
5 Fr.ance
6 Mu.sic
7 Inf.ormation Te.chnology
8 Rel.igion Ed.ucation

	MONDAY	TUESDAY	WEDNESDAY
9–10	Ge ___	Hi ___	Sc ___
10–11	Ma ___	Fr ___	Mu ___
BREAK	////	////	////
11.15–12.15	Inf Te ___	English	Rel Ed ___

79 Education: university

79.1 Complete these definitions of subjects people study at university.

10 marks

1 the study of the human mind and people's behaviour ....

2 the study of how buildings are designed and constructed ....

3 the study of the activities of government ....

4 the study of theories about existence, knowledge and thought ....

5 the scientific study of substances and how they react ....

6 the design and building of machines, roads and bridges ....

7 the study of how to treat illness and injuries ....

8 the study of farming: producing crops and keeping animals ....

9 the study of the rules of a country ....

10 the study of the way society is organised ....

79.2 Write the abbreviations in full. Look at the example first.

4 marks

Example: MPhil stands for ..<u>Master of Philosophy</u>..

1 BA stands for ..<u>Batcitor of Art</u>..

2 BSc stands for ..<u>" science</u>..

3 MA stands for ..<u>Master of Degree</u>..

4 PhD stands for ..<u>pho</u>..

79.3 Complete the text with appropriate verbs in the correct form.

10 marks

When he was 8, my brother's main ambition in life was to
(1)............<u>go</u>............ to university. He was very hard-working
and (2)............<u>get</u>............ well at school. He (3)............<u>took</u>............
three 'A' levels at the age of 18, and fortunately he
(4)............<u>passed</u>.... them all. In fact, he got such high marks
that he managed to (5)...........<u>study</u>.... a place at a very good
university, where he decided to (6)............................ biology.
The course (7)............................ three years, and at the end he
(8)............................ a very good degree. As a result, he got the
chance to go on to postgraduate studies, and he is now
(9)............................ research at Bristol University. Last month
he was asked to (10)............................ a lecture to a group of
young doctors.

79.4 Are these sentences true or false? If they are false, correct them.

6 marks

1 A grant is the money some students receive from a government to pay for education, food
and accommodation.

2 A graduate is someone who has not yet finished their first degree.

3 An MA is a degree that you get on an undergraduate degree course.

4 At university the people who teach you are called lecturers.

5 Tuition is the cost of the teaching of your course.

6 A postgraduate is a second degree course.

Your score

/30

Test your English Vocabulary in Use (pre-intermediate and intermediate)

80 Law and order

80.1
7 marks

Complete the definitions using words in the box.

| jury | attorney | defendant | trial | judge | barrister | accused |

1 This is what takes place in a court of law. A ....
2 The person charged with the crime. The .... or the ....
3 The person who represents people in a higher court of law. In England:
   a .... In the USA: an ....
4 The 12 people who listen to evidence and decide if the person is guilty. The ....
5 The person who decides what sentence a criminal will have. The ....

80.2
7 marks

Correct the mistakes in the <u>underlined</u> parts of the sentences.

1 <u>If you make something illegal</u>, you can get into trouble with the police.
2 If the police believe you have done something wrong, <u>they will make question you</u>.
3 If they know for sure that you did something, <u>they will be charged with the crime</u>.
4 The police may know the person responsible, but <u>it can be hard to prove it on court</u>.
5 Defendants have to prove that <u>they have not guilty</u>.
6 Before they decide, the jury have to <u>listen to all the evidences</u>.
7 <u>At the end of the try</u>, they decide if the person is innocent or not.

80.3
10 marks

Rewrite the sentences using the words on the right (in the correct form) and without changing the meaning. You must also include all the information from the first sentence.

1 The police said he was responsible for the crime.
   The police said .... COMMIT
2 I don't think you have done anything against the law.
   I don't think you .... BREAK
3 I hope the police will try to find out what happened in this case.
   I hope the police .... INVESTIGATE
4 The barrister couldn't provide enough facts to show he was guilty.
   The barrister couldn't .... PROVE
5 In the trial, the jury decided he was guilty of the crime.
   In the trial, he .... CONVICT

80.4
6 marks

Complete these sentences with a suitable word.

1 When someone is guilty, the judge may give that person a prison ....
2 Someone kept in prison is called a ...., and their room is a ....
3 Small crimes like illegal parking are called .... offences and if someone is
   found guilty, the .... will not be prison, but a ...., e.g. £100.

81 Crime

81.1 Complete these sentences using a word from the box.

6 marks

theft	robbery	murder	rape	shoplifting	burglary

1 He was sent to prison for .... after a series of sexual attacks on women.
2 There was a bank .... here last week – they got away with over £1 million.
3 The .... happened during the night while he was away. They broke into the living room and took all the electrical goods.
4 Car .... is one of the most common crimes in our country today.
5 The police found a dead body, but they don't know if it was an accident or ....
6 When the couple were arrested for .... outside the department store, they each were wearing five gold watches.

81.2 Complete the table with the correct word in each space.

6 marks

Crime	Criminal	Crime	Criminal
theft		rape	
robbery		shoplifting	
murder		burglary	

81.3 Replace the underlined word or phrase with a single word.

9 marks

1 The action was against the law, and fortunately he was arrested immediately.
2 The child took the sweets when the shop assistant wasn't looking.
3 To protect your jewellery, it's a good idea to get a strong metal box which is hard to open.
4 We've had a lot of crime in our area, so we've decided to fit a burglar alarm.
5 The police prefer to stop crime before it happens.
6 You shouldn't walk about at night on your own; it's dangerous.
7 He pulled out a knife in an attempt to protect himself from attack.
8 If you want to protect your home and land, you should ask the police for advice.
9 Are the police permitted to carry guns in your country?

81.4 Fill each gap with a suitable word.

9 marks

1 When someone .... a crime, there are many victims.
2 The thieves .... the house and stole money and credit cards.
3 If you are going out in the evening, make sure you leave a light .... and .... the windows and doors.
4 When I go on a trip, I usually wear a .... round my waist to put my passport and cash in.
5 You may need to protect .... at night, and some people use a mace spray.
6 In some countries, there is capital .... for certain crimes such as murder.
7 Killing someone by accident is called ....
8 You have to keep to the .... limit when you are driving in the city.
9 In some parts of town it's dangerous to go out late .... night on your own.

Your score

/30

Test your English Vocabulary in Use (pre-intermediate and intermediate)

82 Politics

82.1 Complete these definitions.

7 marks

1 A state ruled by a king or queen is a ....
2 A state governed by a president and representatives chosen by the people is a
.... People who believe in this are called ....
3 A system of government in which leaders are chosen by the people, e.g. France or the UK,
is called a .... People who believe in this system are ....
4 A state ruled by a single person is a .... The single person who rules is
called a ....

82.2 There are many political beliefs ending in '-ism'. One example is given, but can you write

4 marks down four more?

Example: ..conservatism..

1 ....ism   3 ....ism
2 ....ism   4 ....ism

82.3 Complete these sentences using the correct form of the word on the right.

7 marks

1 He has always held very strong	BELIEVE
2 Why did they .... him?	ELECTION
3 He's the finest .... of his generation.	POLITICS
4 I don't agree with their .... policy.	ECONOMY
5 It was a .... decision.	DEMOCRACY
6 Why does it always become a .... argument?	POLITICS
7 People are still asking the question: who .... the country?	GOVERNMENT

82.4 Complete this text with one word for each gap.

8 marks

The (1)... Minister of
Great Britain has just announced that the general
election will now be
(2)... in four weeks'
time. Most people still believe he will win again,
but it could be close this time. Four years ago his
party won 58% of the
(3)... , and that gave
them over 200 seats in
(4)... , which is fifty
more than all the other parties combined. This
time analysts believe the

(5)... could be as low
as ten, and some people are predicting an even
closer race. There is general agreement that the
government has been successful with its foreign
(6)... , but
unfortunately the economy is still in recession. If
it doesn't improve, there is a possibility that the
government may even lose the
(7)... . It is certainly a
wonderful opportunity for the
(8)... of the opposition
to achieve her greatest ambition.

82.5 Fill the gaps with a single word.

4 marks

1 A: Is Deborah very extreme in her political views?
   B: No, she has always been very middle of the ....
2 Which party is .... power at the moment?
3 It has become quite a right-... party in recent years, although Brian has
   always stayed .... the left of the party.

Your score

/30

83 Bureaucracy

83.1 Match the words with a word from the box to give eight different forms or documents.

8 marks

1 identity ....
2 birth ....
3 driving ....
4 application ....

5 exam ....
6 enrolment ....
7 landing ....
8 TV ....

form
card
certificate
licence

83.2 What are these forms and documents? (Many of them are from 83.1.)

6 marks

1 You fill this in when you are writing off for a job.
2 You may have to fill this in (often on a plane) when you enter another country.
3 This is put in your passport and gives you permission to enter, pass through or leave another country.
4 This card has your name on it and a photo to show who you are.
5 You often fill in one of these before you start a course, e.g. if you study English at a language school.
6 This card states that you are a member of a particular club or organisation.

83.3 Fill the gaps with the best word in these sentences.

4 marks

1 A: I've got a ten-year passport but it .... in two months' time.
   B: But you're planning to go to Venezuela in October, aren't you?
   A: Yes, I am, so I'd better .... it quickly, otherwise I'll be in trouble.
2 A: When I've completed this form, do I have to .... it at the bottom?
   B: Yes, please. Put your .... just there, and next to it put today's date.

83.4 An official is questioning someone who has just arrived in this country. Complete the questions.

4 marks

1 A: .... ?
   B: July 16th, 1980.
2 A: .... ?
   B: Single.
3 A: .... ?
   B: I got here two days ago.
4 A: .... ?
   B: In ten days' time. My flight is on the 21st.

83.5 In written English, the questions in 83.4 are often expressed differently. Complete these expressions.

4 marks

1 Date of ....
2 Marital ....

3 Date of ....
4 Date of ....

83.6 Find words on the right that have the same meaning as the verbs on the left.

4 marks

1 fill in   a stand in line
2 queue   b run out
3 expire   c examine
4 check   d complete

Your score

/30

84.1

8 marks

Replace the <u>underlined</u> words and phrases with a word from the box in the correct form.

defend	conflict	territory	retreat	attack	invade	outbreak	capture

The ⁽¹⁾ <u>strong disagreement</u> over the ⁽²⁾ <u>land belonging to a country</u> in the eastern part of Yarland has led to fighting and the ⁽³⁾ <u>start</u> of war. Yarland has now been ⁽⁴⁾ <u>entered by force</u> by Doeland, and the army has ⁽⁵⁾ <u>taken control of</u> the city of Lugen. The Yarlish soldiers have now ⁽⁶⁾ <u>gone back</u> as far as the border, but the Doe army is still ⁽⁷⁾ <u>taking action to damage</u> the city because there are still small groups of Yarlish fighters who are trying to ⁽⁸⁾ <u>protect</u> it.

84.2

7 marks

Are the <u>underlined</u> words grammatically correct or not? If they are not correct, change them.

1 The <u>armies</u> of many European countries contain <u>troop</u> who are doing military service.
2 The person in charge of the <u>air forces</u> in our country is a woman.
3 The two sides are now in the middle of <u>peace talks</u>.
4 We are hoping the <u>ceasefire</u> will last this time, so that the peace negotiations can continue.
5 We sent <u>aids</u> in the form of medicine and <u>food supply</u>.

84.3

8 marks

What word or phrase is being defined in the sentences below?

1 People who are prepared to take violent action to obtain a political aim. ....
2 People who are taken prisoner by someone who uses them to try to obtain political demands. ....
3 A crime which involves taking control of a means of transport (bus, train or plane) in order to get prisoners. ....
4 People who are not in the army or armed forces. ....
5 An area where there is fighting between two sides. ....
6 To permit a prisoner to go free. ....
7 An official agreement between two sides at the end of a war. ....
8 To fire large guns and explosives at a place. ....

84.4

7 marks

Complete the conversations. You need one word for each gap.

1 A: What happened to the soldiers that were taken by the other side? Are they free now?
  B: Yes, they were .... last night.
2 A: Have they got enough food to last through the winter?
  B: No, the situation is very bad. They have .... everything except rice.
3 A: Is there any news of the soldiers?
  B: Yes – two of them were .... in the fighting and they are in hospital.
4 A: What about the leader? Is he still alive?
  B: No, I don't think so; someone told me he is ....
5 A: I think they are going to propose a ceasefire.
  B: Yes, but I don't think the other side will .... to it.
6 A: You must have been very frightened.
  B: Yes, the soldier .... a gun in the air and everyone ran away.
7 A: Why did they take so many hostages?
  B: So that they could .... for the release of other terrorists.

Pollution and the environment

85.1

10 marks

Fill the gaps to complete these definitions.

1 The air, land and water around us is our ....
2 Dirty air, land and water are all forms of ....
3 The layer of gases which stop dangerous radiation from the sun reaching the earth is called the ....
4 An increase in world temperature which is .... by an increase in carbon dioxide is called ....
5 Rain that contains dangerous chemicals is called ....
6 A place to put your empty bottles is called a bottle ....

85.2

6 marks

Use words from each column to make sentences about how we should help the environment.

Column 1	Column 2	Column 3
Try to	throw away waste save	aluminium cans
	plant	water
Don't	cut down recycle	trees

1 ....
2 ....
3 ....
4 ....
5 ....
6 ....

85.3

8 marks

Complete these sentences using the word on the right in the correct form.

1 Smoke from factories is .... the atmosphere. POLLUTION
2 This is one of many .... problems. ENVIRONMENT
3 Pollution is very .... to people's health. HARM
4 Fortunately there are now many .... groups. CONSERVE
5 Their aim is the .... of all natural things. PROTECT
6 Pollution is .... the environment. DESTRUCTION
7 The effects of this radiation can be very .... DAMAGE
8 .... waste is a big problem. INDUSTRY

85.4

6 marks

Fill the gaps in these sentences with words from the box.

factory	resources	dumping	rain forests	fumes	waste

1 It is very important that we look after natural .... such as water and gas.
2 We need to protect tropical .... such as the Amazon.
3 The company were fined for .... dangerous chemicals straight into the sea.
4 In big cities, two major sources of pollution are car exhaust .... and smoke from .... chimneys.
5 There are strict laws about the disposal of nuclear ....

Your score

/30

Test your English Vocabulary in Use (pre-intermediate and intermediate)

86 Air travel

86.1

5 marks

Replace the underlined words with another word or phrase.

1 The plane's engines started up, and it began to <u>move slowly</u> from the airport building towards the runway.
2 As the passengers were <u>getting on</u> the plane, someone shouted from inside.
3 When he arrived at the desk, the check-in clerk took his <u>suitcases</u> and checked his ticket.
4 The <u>flight attendants</u> were extremely helpful and professional.
5 When we got to Athens, we decided to <u>rent</u> a car for the week.

86.2

8 marks

Match a word from the left with a word from the right to form eight compound nouns.

1 seat   a building   ....
2 seat   b card   ....
3 airline   c luggage   ....
4 boarding   d locker   ....
5 terminal   e representative   ....
6 hand   f number   ....
7 overhead   g baggage   ....
8 excess   h belt   ....

86.3

9 marks

Complete the sentences using a suitable verb.

1 The customs officer .... my passport and gave it back to me. I
   .... through to the departure lounge.
2 A: Do you know your flight times?
   B: Yes, the plane .... off at six in the evening and .... just after ten o'clock.
3 Ladies and gentlemen: would you please .... your seat in the upright position and .... your seat belt. Please extinguish all cigarettes. Thank you.
4 Our flight today will take us over the coast of France and the Bay of Biscay and we will be
   .... at a height of 9000 metres.
5 Unfortunately I had to .... excess baggage and it cost me a fortune.
6 I thought my case was only 15 kg, but when they .... it, it was 23 kg.

86.4

8 marks

Complete the questions.

1 You get lost between leaving the plane and collecting your luggage. You see an official walking down the corridor towards you. What do you ask?
   Excuse me, which way is .... ?
2 You arrive at the airport with your luggage. You are flying American Airlines. What do you ask as soon as you get into the terminal building?
   Excuse me, where is the .... American Airlines?
3 You passed through customs and have been sitting waiting for two hours. Finally, your flight is called and you run to the plane. When you get there, you realise your camera is still where you were sitting. What do you say to the flight attendant?
   Oh, dear, I think I .... lounge.
4 You go to the airport to meet a friend who is arriving from Morocco. When you see them, what do you ask?
   Did .... flight?

Your score

/30

87 Hotels

87.1 Complete these descriptions of hotel accommodation.

8 marks

1 A room for one person with one bed is called a ....

2 A room for two people with one large bed is called a ....

3 A room for two people with two beds is called a ....

4 If you have breakfast, lunch and dinner, it is called ....

87.2 Answer these questions about hotel accommodation in the United Kingdom.

4 marks

1 If a hotel tells you that the room is ensuite, what does that mean?

2 If you decide to have half board at a hotel, what meals are included?

3 If you stayed in a four-star hotel, would it be cheap or expensive?

4 What does B&B stand for?

87.3 Complete these conversations with the correct word.

14 marks

1 GUEST: I'm leaving in ten minutes, so could I pay my .... , please?
RECEPTIONIST: Yes, of course.

2 GUEST: Is breakfast .... in the price of the room?
RECEPTIONIST: No, I'm afraid breakfast is extra.

3 GUEST: .... me. How do I .... to the centre from here?
RECEPTIONIST: Turn right outside the hotel and just keep walking for about ten minutes.

4 GUEST: Are you fully .... next week?
RECEPTIONIST: Yes, I'm afraid we are, sir. It's the middle of the tourist .... so all the hotels are very busy.

5 GUEST: Do you have a .... ?
RECEPTIONIST: I'm sorry sir, we only have the stairs, but I'll take your luggage up for you.

6 GUEST: I'm afraid the central heating in my room isn't .... at all.
RECEPTIONIST: Oh I'm terribly sorry. I'll get someone to look at it.
GUEST: Thank you. Could they also look at the shower? I think there is something .... with it. The water pressure is very low.

7 GUEST: I'd like to leave for the airport in about ten minutes. Could you .... a taxi for me?
RECEPTIONIST: Yes, of course.

8 RECEPTIONIST: Do you already have a reservation?
GUEST: Yes, I .... a room three weeks ago.

9 GUEST: What do I have to do when I arrive?
RECEPTIONIST: Just check in at .... when you get to the hotel.

10 GUEST: Could you give me an early morning .... , please?
RECEPTIONIST: Yes, of course. What time?

11 GUEST: We had an excellent waiter, so I gave him a £10 ....

87.4 What are these people called in a hotel?

4 marks

1 The person who works behind the desk as you enter the hotel.

2 The person who carries luggage to your room.

3 The person who cleans the rooms.

4 The person who cooks the meals in the restaurant.

Your score

/ 30

A sightseeing holiday

88.1 Complete the questions in the dialogue in a suitable way, writing one word for each space.

10 marks

A: Oh, hi, Bill. How was your holiday? Did you (1) .... time?
B: Oh, yes, it was fantastic. Thailand is really beautiful and there is so much to do.
A: Yes, I imagine so. Did you (2) .... of sightseeing, then?
B: Yes, all day long! The temples were incredible.
A: And how about nightlife? Did you (3) .... the evenings?
B: Yes – in fact, we went out every evening to eat and to walk around the streets.
A: But it must have been expensive. Did you (4) .... of money?
B: Yes, I'm sorry to say!
A: So was (5) .... worth .... to Thailand, then?
B: Oh, yes – definitely. It was the holiday of a lifetime.

88.2 Put the letters in the correct order and use the words to label the pictures.

8 marks

celaap   sleact   rat largely   chrealdat
uttsae   tannoufi   karmte   plmtee

1 ....

2 ....

3 ....

4 ....

5 ....

6 ....

7 ....

8 ....

88.3 Which words are being defined here?

7 marks

1 If a place is very crowded and full of people, we can say it is ....
2 If a place has too many tourists, people call it ....
3 To help you remember your holiday, you can buy typical local products which are called
   ....
4 A book which gives you a lot of tourist information about a place is a ....
5 If a place is full of life and activity, we can say it is ....
6 Ancient buildings such as temples, castles and palaces are ....
   ....
7 If a place has a lot of people from different countries and cultures, it is ....

88.4 Put an appropriate verb in the correct form in the gaps.

5 marks

After two weeks in Rome, we spent the last two days in Palermo. We decided to (1)................. a look
round the town immediately. Unfortunately, it was dark, so we (2)................. lost very quickly. Anyway,
the next day, we thought it would be better to (3)................. on a sightseeing tour, which we did.
Anyway, it was the end of a great holiday and we really (4)................. ourselves. I think another time it
would be worth (5)................. a week or two there.

Your score

/30

89 On the beach and in the country

89.1 Complete the gaps. The first letter of each word has been given.

12 marks

Dear Jackie,

We're having a wonderful time! We have found a great (1)p............................... to stay
here in the south of Spain, and we have (2)r............................... a villa with a view of
the sea. The children are particularly enjoying being at the (3)s............................... and
we are (4)s............................... most of our time on the (5)b..............................., which has
beautiful golden (6)s............................... . Poor David is suffering, though. He fell asleep
yesterday while he was (7)s..............................., but he hadn't put any
(8)s............................... l............................... or (9)s............................... on, so he got
(10)s............................... . Today we're going to another (11)r............................... nearby, where
there are some nice fish restaurants and the chance to do (12)v...............................
water sports such as windsurfing and water skiing. Brilliant!
See you soon.

love, Elspeth

89.2 Put the words in these sentences in the correct order.

5 marks

1 a   we   the   go   evenings   stroll   for   in
2 at   get   it   very   to   is   difficult   away   weekends
3 I   to   my   up   and   prefer   nothing   put   feet   do
4 enjoy   really   they   the   and   I   quiet   peace   think
5 are   picnic   we   countryside   have   a   going   the   in   to

5 marks Now match the questions below with a suitable answer from 1–5 above.

a Do you like active or relaxing holidays?
b Have you got any plans for today?
c Why do they spend so much time in the countryside?
d Why don't you come down to the seaside and stay with us on Saturday?
e What do you do after dinner?

89.3 Look at the picture, then complete the text.

8 marks

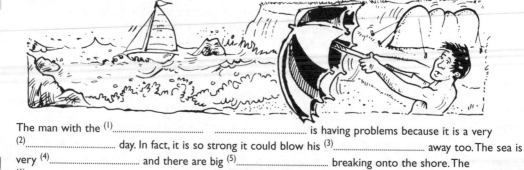

The man with the (1)............................... .... is having problems because it is a very
(2)............................... day. In fact, it is so strong it could blow his (3)............................... away too. The sea is
very (4)............................... and there are big (5)............................... breaking onto the shore. The
(6)............................... is moving dangerously near to the (7)............................... in the sea, just below the
(8)............................... .

Your score

/30

Test your English Vocabulary in Use (pre-intermediate and intermediate)

90.1 Complete the gaps using *in*, *at* or *on*.

10 marks

1 .... *in* .... July		6 .... *in* 2006
2 .... *at* 9.00		7 .... *in* .... the evening
3 .... *on* .... Fridays		8 .... *at* .... Christmas
4 .... *in* .... the afternoon		9 .... *on* .... the last day of the week
5 .... *on* .... the weekend		10 .... *on* .... December 25th

90.2 Are the <u>underlined</u> words correct or not? If they are incorrect, change them.

8 marks

1 I'll wait <u>by</u> he arrives, and then I'll go.
2 Have you seen her <u>since</u> we last met?
3 I have known her <u>during</u> a very long time.
4 They remained calm <u>throughout</u> the negotiations.
5 We fixed the appointment <u>during</u> next Tuesday.
6 I'm seeing him <u>for</u> about a week's time.
7 She met her uncle for the first time <u>during</u> the war.
8 I hope to get to your house <u>by</u> 7.00 at the latest.

90.3 Complete the dialogue using the words or phrases in the box.

5 marks

for ages	for the time being	a long time ago	recently	the other day

A: Where's Emma these days? We had lunch together a few times last month, but I haven't seen her (1)... .

B: She's in Portugal on business. Lucky her!

A: Have you ever been there?

B: Yes, but (2)... . It was before Sam was born and he's nearly ten now. I haven't been anywhere interesting (3)... – it's years since I've been abroad. I'd love to have Emma's job.

A: How's your job going?

B: Well, it's OK (4)... , but if anything better came up, I'd apply for it.

A: There was a great job advertised in the paper (5)... – just right for you.

90.4 Complete the gaps.

3 marks

1 There are 60 *seconds* in a minute.
2 There are 14 days in a *fortnight* .
3 There are 10 years in a *decade* .
4 There are 100 years in a *century* .
5 There are 72 *hours* in three days.
6 There are 1440 *minutes* in a day.

$$\frac{\begin{array}{r} 60 \\ \times 24 \end{array}}{1440}$$

90.5 Put the correct form of *last* or *take*.

4 marks

Your score

/30

1 It usually .... me about 20 minutes to get to work.
2 The interview .... for about an hour – much longer than I expected.
3 How long does it .... to learn English?
4 Fortunately, the cold weather didn't .... long and our holiday was fantastic.

91 | Numbers

91.1 How do you say these numbers in English? Write your answers after each one.

16 marks

Example: 384 __three hundred and eighty-four__

1 212 ....
2 5330 ....
3 3,450,000 ....
4 4.5 ....
5 0.75 ....
6 6.05 ....
7 $3\frac{1}{2}$ ....
8 $12\frac{1}{4}$ ....
9 $1\frac{1}{3}$ ....
10 14 March ....
11 August 21 ....
12 1998 ....
13 1910 ....
14 53% ....
15 603 3579 (phone number) ....
16 −10° ....

91.2 There are four basic processes in arithmetic. The first one has been given, but what are the other three?

3 marks

1 + = addition *Subtraction*
2 − = *Subtractio*

3 × = *Multiply* multipilication
4 ÷ = *Divided* division

91.3 Using only the numbers and symbols in the box, write out the calculations which produce the answers for each number below. There may be more than one way of calculating an answer, but you only need to provide one correct answer in each case.

6 marks

$$\times \quad 80 \quad 2 \quad + \quad 240$$
$$\div \quad 4.5$$
$$128 \quad 4 \quad 12 \quad - \quad 8$$

Example: __Eight times twelve is__ *ninty six* 96

1 6
2 .... 7.5
3 32
4 64
5 512
6 3

91.4 Fill the gaps in these sentences, one word for each gap.

5 marks

1 One, three and five are .... numbers; two, four and six are ....
numbers.

2 More than 50% is the .... ; less than 50% is the ....

Your score

/30

3 If a test has 30 marks and you got 21, you could say this as twenty-one ....
.... thirty.

Distance, size and dimension

92.1 Fill the gaps in these sentences with words from the box.

6 marks

long	far	high	tall

1 A: Is it ....*far*........ to the station?   B: Yes, quite a .... way.
2 A: How ....*tall*........ are you?   B: About one metre seventy-five.
3 A: It'll be a ....*long*........ way, won't it?   B: Yes, too .... to walk, anyway.
4 A: Is it a very ....*high*........ mountain?   B: I've no idea.

92.2 Complete the table.

4 marks

Adjective	Noun	Adjective	Noun
long	*length*	high/tall	*height*
wide	*length*	deep	*depth*

92.3 Using nouns and adjectives from 92.2 (you cannot use the same noun or adjective more than once), write down the dimensions of the field and the swimming pool in the spaces below.

10 marks

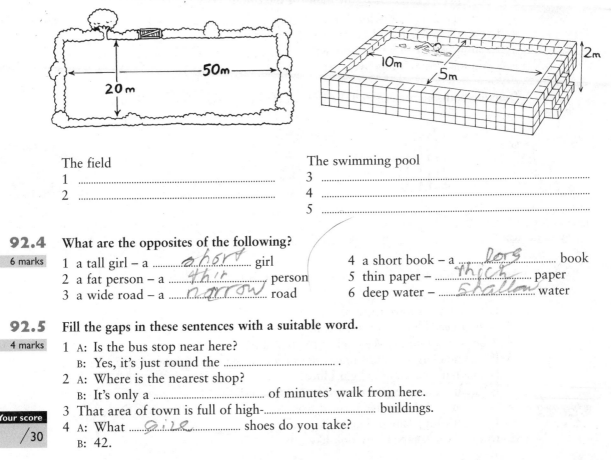

The field
1 ....
2 ....

The swimming pool
3 ....
4 ....
5 ....

92.4 What are the opposites of the following?

6 marks

1 a tall girl – a ....*short*........ girl
2 a fat person – a ....*thin*........ person
3 a wide road – a ....*narrow*........ road
4 a short book – a ....*long*........ book
5 thin paper – ....*thick*........ paper
6 deep water – ....*shallow*........ water

92.5 Fill the gaps in these sentences with a suitable word.

4 marks

1 A: Is the bus stop near here?
   B: Yes, it's just round the ....
2 A: Where is the nearest shop?
   B: It's only a .... of minutes' walk from here.
3 That area of town is full of high-........................... buildings.
4 A: What ....*size*........ shoes do you take?
   B: 42.

Your score

/30

Shapes, colours and patterns

93.1 Label the different shapes.

8 marks

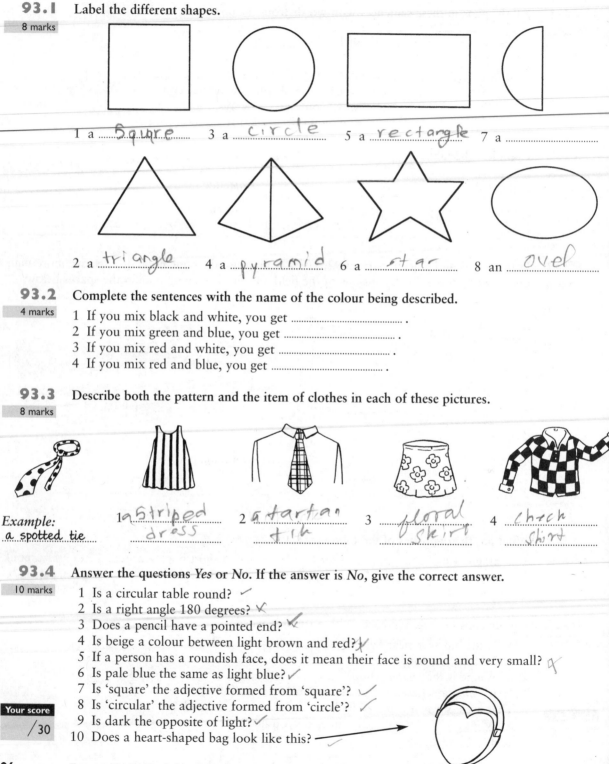

1 a ...*square*... 3 a ...*circle*... 5 a ...*rectangle*... 7 a ....

2 a ...*triangle*... 4 a ...*pyramid*... 6 a ...*star*... 8 an ...*oval*...

93.2 Complete the sentences with the name of the colour being described.

4 marks

1 If you mix black and white, you get ....
2 If you mix green and blue, you get ....
3 If you mix red and white, you get ....
4 If you mix red and blue, you get ....

93.3 Describe both the pattern and the item of clothes in each of these pictures.

8 marks

Example:
a spotted tie

1 a ...*striped dress*... 2 a ...*tartan tie*... 3 ...*floral skirt*... 4 ...*check shirt*...

93.4 Answer the questions *Yes* or *No*. If the answer is *No*, give the correct answer.

10 marks

1 Is a circular table round? ✓
2 Is a right angle 180 degrees? ✗
3 Does a pencil have a pointed end? ✓
4 Is beige a colour between light brown and red? ✗
5 If a person has a roundish face, does it mean their face is round and very small? ✗
6 Is pale blue the same as light blue? ✓
7 Is 'square' the adjective formed from 'square'? ✓
8 Is 'circular' the adjective formed from 'circle'? ✓
9 Is dark the opposite of light? ✓
10 Does a heart-shaped bag look like this? ✓

Your score

/30

Test your English Vocabulary in Use (pre-intermediate and intermediate)

94 Partitives (e.g. *a bowl of, a piece of*)

94.1
2 marks

Here are definitions of two words beginning with the letters 'cont'. What are the words?

1 A cont.................................... is something, such as a box, that can be used for keeping things in.
2 The cont.................................... are the things that you find inside a box, bag, room, etc.

94.2
12 marks

Complete the descriptions under each picture.

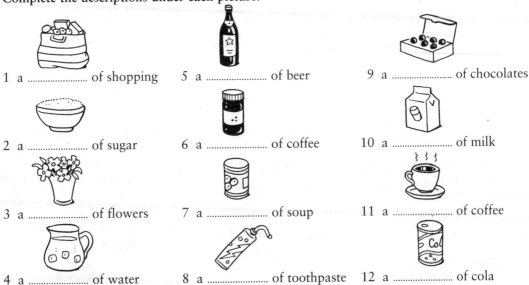

1 a .... of shopping   5 a .... of beer   9 a .... of chocolates

2 a .... of sugar   6 a .... of coffee   10 a .... of milk

3 a .... of flowers   7 a .... of soup   11 a .... of coffee

4 a .... of water   8 a .... of toothpaste   12 a .... of cola

94.3
10 marks

Fill the gaps using the words in the box. You mustn't use any word more than twice.

piece	pair	bit	slice	sheet	bunch

1 We'll need another ....*piece*........ of wood.
2 I only want a .... of butter on my bread.
3 Could I have another .... of paper?
4 How much is that .... of grapes?
5 I'll have to buy another .... of tights.
6 We've still got a .... of time so there's no hurry.
7 If we're going to make sandwiches, we'll need at least ten ....*piece*..........s of bread.
8 Anyone like another .... of cake?
9 I'm just going to put on a clean .... of socks.
10 She gave me a lovely .... of flowers when I was in hospital.

94.4
6 marks

Fill the gaps with a suitable word.

1 You left a .... of cigarettes on the table in the other room.
2 I went on a sailing course and I was with a very interesting .... of people.
3 We opened the gate and there was a great big .... of cows in front of us.
4 Oh, look! $10 on the floor – what a .... of luck!
5 She doesn't like walking through the town centre at night because it is full of .... of teenagers who are looking for trouble.
6 I don't know why she told us that, but it was a useful .... of information.

95.1

10 marks

Fill the gaps with the correct sense word from the box, in the correct form.

look	sound	taste	feel	smell

1 I thought she was English at first, but when she spoke, she .... American.
2 This material is very soft; it almost .... like silk.
3 Did you see those guard dogs? I didn't like the .... of them at all.
4 These flowers .... fantastic; the scent fills the whole room.
5 He said the drink was mostly orange juice, but it didn't .... very nice.
6 When I went into the kitchen there was a strong .... of gas.
7 When he first told me, it .... like a great idea, but I'm not so sure now.
8 I've just had a foot massage. It .... wonderful.
9 That boy .... just like my brother: the same hair and a similar-shaped face.
10 I don't like the .... of this soup; I think it's got too much salt in it.

95.2

5 marks

Complete the sentences with the correct sense verb and a suitable adjective.

1 This girl ....

2 This music ....

3 This bed ....

4 This perfume ....

5 This drink ....

95.3

15 marks

Fill the gaps using verbs from the box, in the correct form.

see	look (at)	watch	hear	listen (to)	press	touch	hold

1 Did you .... that noise?
2 There was a big man standing in front of me so I couldn't .... a thing.
3 I never .... pop music on the radio, except when I'm in the car.
4 The cooker gets very hot, so don't .... it under any circumstances.
5 One of the teachers said she would .... my letter and correct it.
6 My cat loves to sit in the window and .... the birds in the tree outside.
7 I gave the instructions twice, but he still got them wrong; he wasn't ....
8 .... my arm and you won't fall, I promise.
9 We went to the cinema last night to .... that new comedy.
10 I put my money in and .... that button, but nothing happened.
11 I must have .... the wall before the paint was completely dry.
12 If you .... the carpet closely, you can .... how dirty it is.
13 I .... the announcement but I couldn't tell you what he said because I wasn't really ....

Your score

/30

96.1 Complete the signs that are often used in these situations.

10 marks

1 A sign telling people they are not allowed to smoke. NO ....

2 A sign that a hotel guest puts on their door to tell hotel staff not to wake them or go into the room. PLEASE DO NOT ....

3 A sign in the window of a small hotel telling people that the hotel is full. NO ....

4 A notice in a public place, e.g. an airport, asking people to stay on the right and continue on the right. .... RIGHT

5 A notice outside a phone box telling people that it is not working. OUT OF ....

6 A sign people put on a gate, garage door or other entrance, telling motorists not to leave their car there. NO ....

7 The sign that you follow in an airport after you get your luggage if you are not carrying goods you must pay duty on. NOTHING TO ....

8 A notice on a door telling people that they cannot go through this door to leave the building. NO ....

9 A notice outside a cinema or theatre telling people that there are no tickets left. The performance is fully booked. SOLD ....

10 Something people write on a package or parcel to tell the postman that the contents may break easily. ....

96.2 Using all the words once only, make six common signs, notices or warnings.

12 marks

KEEP OFF	SILENCE	OTHER SIDE	NO	PLEASE QUEUE	VACANCIES
IN PROGRESS	YOUR HEAD	DO NOT LEAVE		EXAMINATION	MIND
THE GRASS	BAGS UNATTENDED				

96.3 Complete the warnings.

8 marks

1 Please do not .... the ....

2 Do not .... out of the ....

3 .... the ....

4 .... of ....

97.1 Fill the gaps in these sentences with a suitable noun.

2 marks

1 I have a vague .... of meeting her about five years ago at a conference.

2 I have a vague .... how to get there, but I couldn't give you directions.

97.2 Put either *stuff* or *thing* in the gaps.

7 marks

1 (cream) Is this .... real or artificial?

2 (tomato sauce) My son puts this .... on everything he eats.

3 (cassette player) Does this .... still work?

4 (ink) Be careful with that .... – it stains your hands.

5 (toy) Put that .... down and listen to me.

6 (television) Could you turn that .... off, please? Let's have some peace.

7 (washing up liquid) Can you pass me that .... please?

97.3 Replace 'thing(s)' and 'stuff' in these sentences with suitable nouns.

9 marks

1 You're not going to wear that thing, are you? It doesn't go with your shirt and tie.

2 What's that stuff you're wearing? It smells of lavender.

3 The most important thing to remember is that hotels are very busy, so book in advance.

4 That thing is not meant as a weapon. It's for chopping vegetables, so leave it alone.

5 Does that stuff you're taking really clear your nose and throat?

6 I must write all these things down in my diary before I forget.

7 She's always got so many things in her head; she really is very creative.

8 I tried to ride that thing once but the front wheel came off.

9 Things are going really well – I'm getting married and I've just got a new job.

97.4 There are different words in English meaning 'more or less'. Complete these sentences with three different ones.

3 marks

1 We had to walk .... five kilometres.

2 She was .... twenty minutes late.

3 They're hoping to leave in .... half an hour.

97.5 1 Replace the <u>underlined</u> words with a word from the box.

3 marks

thing	things	stuff

A: What shall I do with this <u>frying pan</u>?

B: It's dirty, isn't it?

A: Yes.

B: Well, could you put it in the dishwasher? It's full, so you could put it on.

A: OK. What shall I use?

B: Oh, the <u>detergent</u> in the bottle under the sink. It's green with a red label.

A: Fine. And how long does it take?

B: An hour. And I just want to iron a few <u>shirts and a tie</u> as well.

6 marks 2 Where in the dialogue could you add the following expressions?

sort of	a bit	roughly

98 American English

98.1

10 marks

Find ten pairs of synonyms (words that mean the same) in the box, then decide which word in each pair is British English and which word is American English. Put your answers in the table below.

lorry	term	gas	lift	car park
main road	trashcan	flat	truck	petrol
cookie	biscuit	dustbin	parking lot	highway
elevator	semester	movie	apartment	film

British English   *American English*

....

....

....

....

....

98.2

10 marks

Label each of the pictures with the correct British English word. Then, under each one, write the American English equivalent.

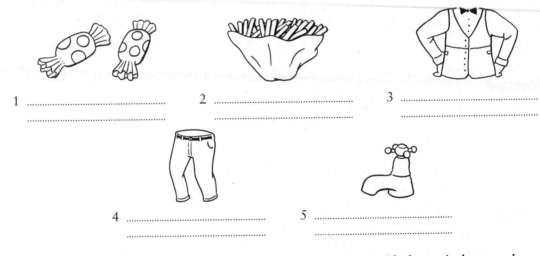

1 ....   2 ....   3 ....

....

4 ....   5 ....

....

98.3

10 marks

Replace the American English word in *italics* in these sentences with the equivalent word used in British English for the same context.

  1 We need to get rid of this *garbage*.
  2 Are you going on *vacation* soon?
  3 Put those things in the *closet*, will you?
  4 It's quicker if you take the *subway*.
  5 Be careful when you step off the *sidewalk*.
  6 Could you get me a packet of *chips*?
  7 I only wear an *undershirt* if it's really cold.
  8 When is your daughter starting *high school*?
  9 We're going to spend a few days there in the *fall*.
 10 I think I'd better buy a *round trip*.

99 Formal and informal English

99.1

7 marks

The first line in each situation below is in formal English, and the second line expresses the same meaning in more informal English. Fill the gaps with appropriate words, but do not repeat words already used in the first sentences.

1 A LETTER

I .... to .... you that we are .... to offer

you any more ...

I am sorry to say that we can't offer you any more ...

2 SIGN IN CAFE

Only food .... here may be consumed on the ....

Only food bought here can be eaten here (in the cafe).

3

If you .... any further .... , please remember to ...

If you need any more help, please remember to ...

99.2

5 marks

Replace the words in *italics* with a <u>less formal</u> alternative that has the same meaning.

1 This is for hotel *patrons* only.
2 I believe it is due to *commence* in ten minutes.
3 They've taken a break for lunch but I understand the meeting will *resume* afterwards if there are further issues to discuss.
4 Where was this man *apprehended*?
5 It was dark at the time, *thus* the witness was unable to identify the man.

99.3

12 marks

Replace the word in *italics* with a <u>less informal</u> alternative that has the same meaning.

1 His last film was *terrific*.
2 She is one of the *brightest* students in the class.
3 When can I *pick up* the photos?
4 I got it for twenty *quid* in the end.
5 Did you manage to *fix up* a meeting for next week?
6 I'm going to the *loo*. I won't be a minute.
7 They should be here *pretty* soon.
8 Where have the *kids* gone?
9 This place is very *handy* for the underground.
10 What time do you *reckon* we should leave?
11 He's a very nice *guy*.
12 What time did you *get there*?

99.4

6 marks

Rewrite these sentences in less formal English by including the words on the right. Add or change any words that are necessary, but keep the meaning the same.

1 Would you like to go out? ....
  Do ....?   FANCY
2 We must contact them soon. ....
  We ....   TOUCH
3 I'm going to talk to him. ....
  I'm going ....   A WORD

Abbreviations and abbreviated words

100.1

8 marks

What do these abbreviations stand for?

1 UK = ...
2 UN = ...
3 BBC = ...
4 PM = ...
5 MP = ... of ....
6 EU = ...
7 VAT = ...
8 asap = ...

100.2

6 marks

Answer these questions.

1 There is a special abbreviation used to describe an organisation of the countries that export oil. What is the abbreviation?
2 There is also an abbreviation to describe the very serious illness that develops from the HIV virus. What is it?
3 We use the written abbreviation *Mrs* for a married woman. What abbreviation can we also use for a woman that does not specify whether she is marrried or single?
4 The abbreviation *St* can have two meanings. What are they?
5 What written abbreviation is used for 'Doctor'?
6 People often talk about their PC, but what exactly are they referring to?

100.3

6 marks

How would we express these written abbreviations in spoken English?

1 etc. = and ....
2 e.g. = ...
3 i.e. = ... words

100.4

10 marks

Some English words are often shortened, e.g. 'telephone' to 'phone'. In the following sentences find other words that can also be shortened, <u>underline</u> them, and then write the short form at the end of the sentence.

Example: Could you help me with my <u>suitcase</u>? It's very heavy.   *case*

1 When did your brother decide that he wanted to become a veterinary surgeon?
2 I've got a very nice photograph of the team which was taken just after they won the cup.
3 If I were you, I'd put an advertisement in the local paper and see what response you get.
4 People often say they've got influenza when, in fact, they've got nothing more than a common cold.
5 The trouble with our teacher is that she puts things on the blackboard then rubs it off before we've had time to write it all down.
6 There should be some butter on the table, but if not, get some from the refrigerator.
7 I think Pete must be mad to ride his bicycle through central London during the rush hour.
8 He's down in the laboratory, doing an experiment.
9 He's a sales representative for a big pharmaceutical company.
10 They went by aeroplane but came back in a helicopter.

Your score

/30

Answer key

Notes on the answer key and marking

1 Each test has a total of 30 marks.

2 There is one mark for each correct answer in most exercises. Sometimes there is half a mark or two marks for each correct answer. You will find the total marks for each exercise below the exercise number on the test page, and on the right hand side in the answer key.

3 If two answers are given in the key (separated by a slash /), both answers are correct.

   Example: Remove writing from the board = ... it off
            Answer: rub/clean

4 Words which are particularly difficult to pronounce are given in phonetic script in the Answer key. Words which cause difficulties with word stress have the stressed syllable in **bold** print.

Tests 1–3

1–3.1   (5 marks)

1–3.2   1 lost   2 dirty   3 fall   4 rude/impolite   5 ugly /ˈʌglɪ/   (5 marks)

1–3.3   1 put on: weight /weɪt/, your gloves   3 do: homework, an exercise
             2 take: half an hour, a photo   4 make: a mistake, a mess   (4 marks)

1–3.4   1 without a noise   2 a lot   3 study it again   4 is
             5 unhappy because you are away from home   (5 marks)

1–3.5

Verb	Noun
ex**plain**	explanation
choose	choice
de**fine**	definition
trans**late**	translation
pro**nounce**	pronunciation

                                                                    (5 marks)

1–3.6   1 different   2 same   3 same   4 different   5 different   6 same   (6 marks)

Test 4

4.1   1 noun   4 preposition   7 noun   10 pronoun
       2 definite article   5 adjective   8 adverb   11 preposition
       3 verb   6 indefinite article   9 adjective   12 verb   (12 marks)

4.2   1 an uncountable noun   3 an uncountable noun   5 an infinitive
       2 a plural noun   4 phrasal verbs   6 an idiom   (6 marks)

4.3 1 **pre**fix   3 synonym   5 phonetic   7 stress
       2 **suf**fix   4 opposite   6 syllables (twice)   (7 marks)

4.4 1 full stop   2 question mark   3 comma   4 brackets   5 hyphen   (5 marks)

Test 5

5.1 enough /ɪˈnʌf/ – trouble /ˈtrʌbl/; cough /kɒf/ – hot; diet /ˈdaɪət/ – island /ˈaɪlənd/;
       since /sɪns/ – opposite /ˈɒpəzɪt/; police /pəˈliːs/ – machine /məˈʃiːn/;
       accent /ˈæksənt/ – palace /ˈpælɪs/; potato /pəˈteɪtəʊ/ – razor /ˈreɪzə/;
       calm /kaːm/ – fast /faːst/   (8 marks)

5.2 1 pre**fer**   3 **or**ganise   5 ma**chine**
       2 under**stand**   4 **hy**phen   6 compe**ti**tion   (6 marks)

5.3 1 /rɪst/   3 /ˈɒnɪst/   5 /bɒm/   7 /ˈfaːsən/   9 /ˈkrɪsməs/
       2 /aɪl/   4 /niː/   6 /ˈhænsəm/ 8 /naɪf/   (9 marks)

5.4 1 isl(a)nd /ˈaɪlənd/   4 cin(e)ma /ˈsɪnəmə/   7 pil(o)t /ˈpaɪlət/
       2 sciss(o)rs /ˈsɪzəs/   5 raz(o)r /ˈreɪzə/
       3 p(o)tatoes /pəˈteɪtəʊz/   6 bac(o)n /ˈbeɪkən/   (7 marks)

Test 6

6.1 1 **vid**eo cas**sette**   3 **pho**tocopier   5 **o**verhead pro**jec**tor
       2 **pen**cil **shar**pener   4 cas**sette** re**cor**der   6 **hole** punch   (6 marks)

6.2 1 look it up   3 rub/clean   5 turn it up
       2 borrow   4 repeat   6 swap   (6 marks)

6.3 You put an *OHT* on an *OHP*.
       You put a *plug* /plʌg/ in a *socket*.
       You use *chalk* /tʃɔːk/ to write on a *board*.
       You put a *file* /faɪl/ in a *briefcase*.   (8 marks)

6.4 1 down   2 plug   3 correct   4 rubber/eraser   (4 marks)

6.5 1 What does 'damage' mean?
       2 How do you spell 'X'?
       3 How do you pronounce 'bicycle'?   (6 marks)

Test 7

7.1 1 un**frien**dly   4 in**vis**ible   7 irre**spon**sible   10 im**poss**ible
       2 il**leg**ible   5 ir**reg**ular   8 in**cor**rect
       3 unem**ployed**   6 im**pa**tient   9 dis**hon**est   (10 marks)

7.2 1 il**leg**al   3 disa**gree**   5 dis**likes**
       2 un**dress**   4 un**ti**dy   6 im**po**lite   (6 marks)

7.3 1 re-   2 mis-   3 un-, dis-   4 over-   (5 marks)

7.4 1 misunderstood   4 misheard   7 unlock
       2 oversleep   5 reopen   8 overcharged
       3 unpack   6 disappeared   9 redo /riːˈduː/   (9 marks)

Test 8

8.1
1 discussion	4 election	7 similarity	10 **dark**ness
2 punctuality	5 **spelling**	8 im**prove**ment	
3 organisation	6 **happiness**	9 information	(10 marks)

8.2
1 stupid	3 improve	5 elect	7 artist
2 jogging	4 discuss	6 punctual	

The vertical word is 'similar', and its opposite is 'different'. (8 marks)

8.3

Verb	General noun	Adjective	General noun
educate	education	popular	popularity
manage	**man**agement	weak	**weak**ness
translate	translation	stupid	stu**pid**ity
hesitate	hesitation		

$\frac{1}{2}$ mark for the correct word, $\frac{1}{2}$ for the correct stress) (6 marks:

8.4
1 **mur**derer /'mɜːdərə/	5 translator	9 **op**erator
2 actor	6 em**ploy**er	10 **foot**baller
3 economist	7 psy**chol**ogist	11 **film** director
4 **farm**er	8 **singer**	12 **jour**nalist/re**por**ter (6 marks)

Test 9

9.1
1 inedible	4 un**suit**able	7 re**li**able /rɪ'laɪəbl/
2 un**drink**able	5 en**joy**able	8 incompre**hens**ible
3 com**fort**able	6 **flex**ible	9 un**break**able (9 marks)

9.2 1 useless   2 painless   3 homeless   4 careless   5 thoughtless   (5 marks)

9.3
1 musical	3 washable	5 political	7 attractive
2 economical	4 knowledgeable /'nɒlɪdʒəbl/	6 creative	(7 marks)

9.4
1 It is too cloudy to see the stars tonight.
2 If it is still foggy in an hour, we will have to cancel the trip.
3 It's a very industrial town.
4 That corner of the room is very dirty.
5 She knows that drugs are dangerous. (5 marks)

9.5 painful   helpful   thoughtful   careful (4 marks)

Test 10

10.1
1 smile	3 pull	5 ache /eɪk/	7 laugh /lɑːf/
2 dream	4 queue /kjuː/	6 clean	8 taste (8 marks)

'Clean' can also be used as an adjective. (1 mark)

10.2 1 b   2 f   3 a   4 e   5 d   6 c (6 marks)

'Dry' can also be used as an adjective. (1 mark)

10.3
1 Did you send a reply to the invitation?
2 Could you have a look at this report for me?
3 People go on (a) diet/diets /'daɪət/ for all sorts of reasons.
4 If you don't know the answer, just have a guess.
5 Someone gave me a push and I fell over.
6 We had to wait in a/the queue for ages.
7 Why don't you give her a ring when she gets back? (14 marks)

Test 11

11.1 1 **mother** tongue   4 **baby**-sitter   7 **in**come tax
2 science **fiction**   5 **traffic** jam   8 **brother**-in-law
3 **box** office   6 **dining** room   (8 marks)

11.2 1 **traffic** lights   3 **earrings**   5 **cred**it card   7 T-shirt
2 **sun**glasses   4 **alarm** clock   6 **tin** opener   8 pede**strian** **crossing**   (8 marks)

11.3 1 jam, congestion, warden
2 post, ticket
3 dining, living, sitting, waiting, bath, spare
4 sister, mother, father, son, daughter   (4 marks:
$\frac{1}{2}$ for each correct answer)

11.4 1 first **aid**   3 **film** star   5 **park**ing meter
2 **cheque** book   4 **wash**ing machine   6 **writ**ing paper   (6 marks)

11.5 1 **pop/rock** stars   3 **hair**dryer (or hair drier)
2 toothpaste /ˈtuːθpeɪst/   4 **table** tennis   (4 marks)

Test 12

12.1 1 well-known   3 badly-paid   5 badly-off   7 well-dressed
2 good-looking   4 easy-going   6 full-time   8 well-behaved   (8 marks)

12.2 1 I found a fifty-dollar bill in the street yesterday. / Yesterday I found a fifty-dollar bill in the street.
2 It is only a ten-minute drive to my office.
3 Unfortunately we had a three-hour delay at the airport (unfortunately).
4 Movie stars often stay in five-star hotels.
5 You can't expect a three-year-old child to understand.   (5 marks)

12.3 1 part-time   4 brand-new   7 well-behaved   10 badly-paid
2 easy-going   5 four-month-old   8 south-west
3 well-off   6 six-year-old   9 five-minute   (10 marks)

12.4 1 second-hand; badly-made   3 left-handed   5 first-class
2 well-acted; badly-directed   4 short-sleeved   (7 marks)

Test 13

13.1 1 He *missed* the bus   5 *broad* shoulders
2 I *make* a lot of mistakes   6 Don't *get in* the car
3 she *told* a lie   7 My father *tells*
4 I *missed* the lesson   8 a *serious* illness   (8 marks)

13.2 1 aware /əˈweə/   4 success /səkˈses/   7 important
2 unlikely /ʌnˈlaɪkli/   5 range
3 work   6 majority /məˈdʒɒrəti/   (7 marks)

13.3 1 false (the opposite of a dry wine is a sweet wine)
2 true
3 true
4 false (the opposite of a soft drink is an alcoholic drink)

5 true
6 false (the opposite of a strong accent is a slight accent)
7 false (the opposite of a light smoker is a heavy smoker)
8 true   (8 marks)

13.4 The following are *not* correct:

1 to start a bicycle	4 all correct	7 to run a joke
2 a heavy lesson	5 to get on/off a taxi	
3 get into/out of a bike	6 all correct	(7 marks)

Test 14

14.1

1 listening *to* the radio	6 suffering *from* shock
2 it depends *on* the weather	7 apply *for* that job
3 different *from*	8 good *at* maths
4 shouted *at* me	9 waiting *for* a call
5 interested *in* sport	10 spending money *on* things (10 marks)

14.2

1 at	3 of	5 with	7 to
2 to	4 at/by	6 of	8 to (8 marks)

14.3
1 She apologised for the mistake.
2 I agree with you.
3 This car belongs to me.
4 He is aware of the problem.
5 This book is similar to the other one.
6 I am not very keen on football.   (12 marks)

Test 15

15.1

1 by	3 in	5 on	7 by	9 in	11 for
2 on	4 by	6 in, for	8 by	10 at	(12 marks)

15.2

1 on holiday	5 by chance
2 by accident; on purpose /'pɜːpəs/	6 on my own
3 on strike /straɪk/	7 on foot (8 marks)
4 by mistake (by accident is possible)	

15.3 1 on time   2 in time   3 at least   4 out of work   (4 marks)

15.4

1 on business	3 in a moment	5 at the end
2 in the end	4 on the radio	6 in business (6 marks)

Test 16

16.1

1 up	3 up	5 down	7 down/over	9 off
2 up; off	4 out	6 up	8 up	10 up; down (12 marks)

16.2 1 c   2 c   3 a   4 d   5 c   (5 marks)

16.3

1 look it up	3 gave it up	5 get through	7 get on ... with (8 marks)
2 carry on	4 pick it up	6 takes off	8 run out of

16.4

1 pick up	3 get through	5 go off
2 went off	4 take off	(5 marks)

Test 17

17.1
1 *got off* the train 4 *stay in* this weekend 7 correct
2 correct 5 *growing up* quickly 8 *woke up* at
3 put *them on* 6 correct (8 marks)

17.2
1 The plane is taking off.
2 The woman is getting off the bus.
3 He/She is putting out a/his/her cigarette / is putting his/her cigarette out.
4 The car has broken down.
5 The dog is lying (down) in front of the fire.
6 The woman is picking/tidying up the toys. (12 marks)

17.3
1 turn over 4 make it up 7 came/went in 10 get by
2 find out 5 broke into 8 gone up
3 turn up 6 broke down 9 leave/miss out (10 marks)

Test 18

18.1
1 e 2 d 3 h 4 g 5 f 6 c 7 b 8 a (8 marks)

18.2
1 pulling ... leg 3 get ... move 5 make ... mind
2 keep ... eye 4 make matters 6 take ... turns (12 marks)

18.3
1 mad 2 time 3 cut 4 good 5 nerves (5 marks)

18.4
1 small 2 offhand 3 long 4 for 5 up (5 marks)

Test 19

19.1
1 had 3 take 5 have/take 7 have
2 make 4 have 6 do 8 do (8 marks)

19.2
1 do any housework/cleaning 5 making so much noise
2 make mistakes 6 doing research
3 subjects do you do 7 making really good progress / doing really good work
4 did two exams (14 marks)

19.3
1 homework 2 a noise 3 research 4 a mistake (4 marks)

19.4
1 hungry 2 thirsty 3 to have a baby 4 time in Brazil (4 marks)

Test 20

20.1
1 give me a hand 5 breaks the law
2 catch the train 6 keep breaking glasses
3 keep your hands warm 7 ball; catch
4 caught a cold 8 keep a record (16 marks)

20.2
1 keep in touch /tʌtʃ/ 3 give my regards
2 break the ice 4 see the point of/in (8 marks)

20.3
1 see 3 see 5 give
2 keep 4 break 6 keep (6 marks)

Test 21

21.1 1 receive   5 reach/arrive   9 obtain
       2 reach/arrive   6 obtain   10 fetch / go and bring back
       3 fetch / go and bring back   7 become
       4 become   8 receive   (10 marks)

21.2 1 get dressed   4 get lost
       2 get undressed   5 get divorced
       3 get changed   6 get married   (6 marks)

21.3 1 g   2 a   3 d   4 b   5 f   6 c   7 h   8 e   (8 marks)

21.4 1 get on (well)   3 get to know   5 getting up
       2 you getting on   4 get rid of   6 get ready   (6 marks)

Test 22

22.1 1 deaf   3 bankrupt   5 yellow/red/brown
       2 bald /bɔːld/   4 mad   6 grey   (6 marks)

22.2 1 They're going shopping.
       2 They're going walking/hiking. / They're going for a walk.
       3 They're going sightseeing.
       4 They're going swimming / for a swim.
       5 They're going skiing.
       6 They're going (out) for a drive.
       7 They're going riding / (out) for a ride.
       8 They're going running / for a run.   (8 marks)

22.3 1 d   2 f   3 e   4 g   5 a   6 c   7 b   (7 marks)

22.4 1 come   3 come   5 come   7 take   9 go
       2 bring   4 take   6 take   8 comes   (9 marks)

Test 23

23.1 1 I'm late / for being late   4 apologise /əˈpɒlədʒaɪz/ for being
       2 beg   5 accept our apology (apologies) /əˈpɒlədʒɪz/
       3 keep ... long   (8 marks)

23.2 1 Yes, they were delayed.
       2 It's OK, I'll / I'm going to clear it up.
       3 Yes, we can sort them out.
       4 They were, but several people were ill so they had to cancel it.   (8 marks)

23.3 Don't worry   Never mind   It doesn't matter   No problem   (4 marks)

23.4 ... sorry *about* the mess
       ... clear it *up*
       ... kind *of* you
       ... thanks *a* lot   (8 marks)

23.5 hospitality   (2 marks)

Test 24

24.1
1 A: Could *I* borrow *a/your* pen *for* five minutes?
   B: Yes, *help* yourself.
2 A: Could *you* give *me* that book *over* there?
   B: Yes, *of* course. Here you are.
3 A: I *was* wondering *if* I *could* use your bike for half an hour?
   B: Well, I'd rather *you* didn't actually. I may need it myself.
4 A: Do you *think* you could *possibly* lend *me* some CDs?
   B: I *wish* I could, but I haven't got any.
5 A: Mary, *would* you like *to* go *out* this evening?
   B: I'd love *to* but I'm *afraid* I can't.
6 A: Would you *mind* if I *took/had* the afternoon off? I don't feel very well.
7 A: Can *you* give *me* a hand?   (15 marks:
   B: I'm afraid *not*, just at the moment. I have *to* go out.   ½ for each gap)

24.2 1 that's / what   2 if   3 mind /maɪnd/   4 on/with   5 sorry   (5 marks)

24.3 A: What *shall we* do at the weekend?
          B: Uh, let me think. OK, *how about going* to the beach?
          A: Yeah, great. And *this evening*? Do you want to see that film?
          B: I think *I'd prefer to* stay in actually.
          A: Yes, OK, *I don't mind*.   (10 marks)

Test 25

25.1
1 What do you think *of/about* ...
2 I *don't think* it's a good idea.
3 In my *opinion*, ...
4 I'm afraid ... (omit *but*)
5 ... I *totally* disagree
6 Yes, it *says* in one newspaper that ... / *according to* one newspaper, most people ...
7 You *could/may* be right ...
8 Yes, *I agree* ...   (8 marks)

25.2 The correct order is: d, f, c, e, b, a   (6 marks)

25.3
1 What are your feelings about his new plan?
2 Well, as far as I'm concerned, more people should go to university.
3 You know, according to the paper, he's still missing.
4 I think you're right.
5 I agree with you to some extent / to a certain extent.   (10 marks)

25.4
1 What do you think / What's your (honest) opinion
2 personally
3 agree
4 some extent / a certain extent
5 according to
6 don't think that's / can't believe that's   (6 marks)

Test 26

26.1 1 Good evening
          2 How do you do / Pleased to meet you / Hello.

3 correct
4 Yes, same to you / Yes, you too.
5 correct
6 correct – 'bad luck' would also be correct (6 marks)

26.2 1 Good luck 3 Bless you; Thank you 5 Watch/Look 7 Happy New
2 Cheers /'tʃɪəz/ 4 Excuse me 6 idea (8 marks)

26.3 1 done 2 met you 3 pardon 4 going (4 marks)

26.4 1 false (we don't say 'How are you?')
2 true
3 false ('Cheerio' /tʃɪrɪ'əʊ/ is another way of saying 'Goodbye')
4 true
5 true
6 false (in the afternoon they say 'Good afternoon', not 'Good day')
7 true (some people, especially waiters in restaurants, are now in the habit of saying 'Enjoy your meal', but it is not a common expression)
8 false (we can say 'Merry Christmas' or 'Happy Christmas' but not 'Merry Birthday'; the correct expression is 'Happy Birthday') (12 marks)

Test 27

27.1 1 true
2 true
3 false (they can be used with 'the', but not with the *in*definite article 'a/an')
4 true
5 false (they are used with a plural verb) (5 marks)

27.2 1 information 3 good weather 5 my hair is
2 any work 4 a new pair of trousers 6 housework (6 marks)

27.3 1 I don't usually take much luggage /'lʌɡɪdʒ/ with me.
2 Her teacher sometimes gives her a lot of homework (to do) in the evening.
3 She's definitely making progress.
4 He gave me a lot of advice.
5 I only have a little knowledge of Spanish.
6 I'm going to buy a pair of jeans. (12 marks)

27.4 1 sunglasses 3 scales /skeɪlz/ 5 stairs 7 headphones
2 shorts 4 scissors /'sɪzəz/ 6 pyjamas /pɪ'dʒɑːməz/ (7 marks)

Test 28

28.1 Verbs + -ing: finish, imagine, avoid, admit
Verbs + infinitive: hope, refuse, decide, seem (8 marks)

28.2 Correct answers are:
1 a, b 3 a, c 5 a, b
2 b, c 4 b, c 6 a, c (6 marks)

28.3 1 give up 3 manage /'mænɪdʒ/ 5 make 7 let
2 can't stand 4 deny 6 remember 8 allow (8 marks)

28.4 1 He enjoys playing football, but he doesn't expect to get a place on the team.
2 He admits taking the money, but he denies hitting the guard.
3 She (has) offered to help us today, but she (has) refused to come tomorrow.   (8 marks:
4 I feel like going out, but my parents won't let me use the car.   2 for each sentence)

Test 29

29.1 1 insist   3 blame   5 warn /wɔːn/
2 persuade /pəˈsweɪd/   4 apologise   6 complain   (6 marks)

29.2 1 She told me the course was/had been a waste of time.
2 She asked me to leave by the side door.
3 She advised me to buy another one.
4 She suggested (that) we do / did / should do the exercise later OR She suggested doing the exercise later.
5 She warned me not to go near the rocks.
6 She insisted that I don't/didn't tell anyone.   (12 marks)

29.3 1 incorrect   4 incorrect   7 incorrect
2 incorrect   5 correct   8 correct
3 correct   6 incorrect   (8 marks)

29.4 1 for   2 on   3 for   4 about   (4 marks)

Test 30

30.1

big	huge /hjuːdʒ/, enormous
interesting /ˈɪntrəstɪŋ/	fascinating
surprised	astonished, amazed
hot	boiling
cold	freezing
crowded	packed
small	tiny /ˈtaɪni/, minute /maɪˈnjuːt/
hungry	starving
tired	exhausted /ɪgˈzɔːstɪd/
frightened /ˈfraɪtənd/	terrified (10 marks)

30.2 1 packed   4 huge/enormous
2 starving   5 awful/terrible/dreadful /ˈdredfəl/
3 freezing; boiling (either order is possible)   (6 marks)

30.3 1 terrifying   3 huge   5 excited   7 absolutely   9 fascinating
2 terrific   4 embarrassed 6 astonished   8 tiring   (9 marks)

30.4 1 Her results were disappointing.
2 I was confused by the map.
3 The sales figures were depressing.
4 She was really frightened by the film.
5 The climb was exhausting.   (5 marks)

Test 31

31.1 1 correct   4 correct   7 in your pocket   10 in the garden
2 on the table   5 in a very nice area 8 correct
3 at work   6 at the party   9 at the table   (10 marks)

31.2
1 up	4 below/beneath	7 in front of	10 over
2 out of	5 behind	8 up	
3 over	6 out of	9 below/beneath	(10 marks)

31.3
1 toward(s)	4 opposite	7 along/beside
2 next to / beside	5 across	8 round/past; through /θru:/ /across
3 between	6 past	9 near (10 marks)

Test 32

32.1   1 Yes   2 No   3 No   4 Yes   5 No   6 Yes   7 Yes   (7 marks)

32.2   regularly   sometimes   occasionally /ə'keɪʒənəli/   hardly ever   (4 marks)

32.3   1 He is hardly ever late for work.
2 We occasionally take the children to the pool. (*Occasionally* can go at the beginning or the end of the sentence.)
3 She has always stayed in the same hotel.
4 I quite often forget to lock the door.
5 You can rarely find fresh fish in the market.   (5 marks)

32.4
1 We were a bit tired.	5 I find it quite boring.
2 It was pretty good.	6 It's quite the same as yours.
3 The film was rather interesting.	7 I seldom see him.
4 We had a pretty good time.	(7 marks)

32.5
1 was *hardly* enough room	5 father *nearly* forgot
2 we *barely* /ˈbeəli/ had time	6 was *a bit* shocked
3 was *almost* dark	7 brother *hardly ever* comes
4 were *incredibly* tired	(7 marks)

Test 33

33.1
1 when, as soon as	4 as, just as	7 while
2 while	5 when, as soon as	
3 when, while	6 when, while	(12 marks)

33.2
1 first of all / first(ly)	3 after that / then
2 then / after that	4 finally (4 marks)

33.3   1 Yes   2 Yes   3 No   4 No   5 Yes   6 Yes   (6 marks)

33.4   1 for one thing; for another
2 to start/begin with; and besides/anyway   (8 marks)

Test 34

34.1
1 whereas /weə'ræz/	6 while/whilst/but
2 as well	7 too
3 although /ɔ:l'ðəʊ/	8 though / even though / but
4 however	9 on the other hand
5 furthermore /fɜ:ðə'mɔ:/	10 in addition / what's more / moreover /mɔ:'rəʊvə/ also (10 marks)

34.2   1 c   2 b   3 b   4 a   5 c   6 a   7 b   8 a   (8 marks)

34.3 1 whereas/while 4 Furthermore / What's more / In addition
2 however 5 on the other hand / however
3 despite /dɪˈspaɪt/ / in spite of 6 although (12 marks)

Test 35

35.1 1 Anne is similar to Barbara.
2 Diana and Claire are quite alike /əˈlaɪk/.
3 Barbara is quite unlike Claire.
4 Anne is very different from Diana, except that they both have wavy hair.
5 Neither Anne nor Barbara has short hair. (7 marks)

35.2 1 You'll lose your umbrella unless you keep it in your bag.
2 I think you'll pass the test as long as you don't get too nervous.
3 You'd better take some money in case you have to take a taxi.
4 You should leave by 7.00 otherwise you'll miss the bus.
5 You look the same as usual except that you're wearing glasses. (10 marks)

35.3 1 the same meaning 4 different 7 the same meaning
2 the same meaning 5 the same meaning 8 different
3 different 6 different (8 marks)

35.4 1 nothing/little 4 unless
2 compared / in comparison 5 or/otherwise /ˈʌðəwaɪz/
3 except (for) / apart from (5 marks)

Test 36

36.1 1 I lost my wallet so I had to borrow some money.
2 I went to the post office because I needed some stamps.
3 I had to stop the traffic because of the accident.
4 I stayed at work late so that I could finish the report.
5 My wife is very ill and therefore I have given up work to look after her.
6 I couldn't got to the meeting. Consequently, I learnt the bad news much later. (12 marks)

36.2 1 a 2 a 3 b 4 a 5 b 6 a (6 marks)

36.3 1 As 3 As a result 5 Consequently 7 because
2 Owing to 4 because of 6 because of (7 marks)

36.4 1 as 2 Consequently 3 due to 4 and therefore 5 so that (5 marks)

Test 37

37.1 1 group of islands 5 desert /ˈdezət/ 9 continent
2 mountain range 6 Lake 10 country
3 river 7 ocean /ˈəʊʃən/ 11 jungle /dʒʌŋgl/
4 island /ˈaɪlənd/ 8 mountain /ˈmaʊntɪn/ 12 Sea (12 marks)

37.2 1 Earth 3 Poles 5 equator
2 Falls 4 stars 6 moon (6 marks)

37.3 1 – 2 – 3 the 4 the 5 the 6 – (6 marks)

37.4 1 drought 3 flood 5 hurricane /ˈhʌrɪkən/
2 volcanic eruption 4 earthquake 6 disasters (6 marks)

Test 38

38.1

Noun	Adjective	Noun	Adjective
sun	sunny	wind	windy /ˈwɪndi/
cloud	cloudy	fog	foggy
ice	ic(e)y	heat	hot
shower	showery	humidity	humid

(8 marks)

38.2 (1) boiling – hot – warm – not very warm – chilly – freezing (6)   (3 marks)

(1) a breeze – a wind – a gale – a hurricane /ˈhʌrɪkən/ (4)   (2 marks)

38.3
1 heavy rain
2 strong wind
3 thunder /ˈθʌndə/ and lightning /ˈlaɪtnɪŋ/
4 pouring /ˈpɔːrɪŋ/ with rain
5 a spell/period of hot weather
6 blew   (6 marks)

38.4
1 foggy
2 ic(e)y
3 temperature
4 showers
5 hurricanes
6 (thunder)storm
7 minus /ˈmaɪnəs/; zero / freezing point
8 breeze
9 humidity
10 cloudy   (11 marks)

Test 39

39.1 1 leaves   2 branch   3 roots   4 soil/ground   5 grass   6 plants/flowers (6 marks)

39.2
1 farm
2 agriculture /ˈægrɪkʌltʃə/
3 keeps
4 slaughtered /ˈslɔːtəd/
5 dairy
6 crops
7 grew
8 planted
9 pick
10 harvest
11 drought /draʊt/
12 ground
13 water   (13 marks)

39.3
1 copper
2 ground
3 metals
4 valuable /ˈvæljuːəbl/
5 mine
6 iron /ˈaɪən/
7 tin
8 silver
9 coins
10 gold

The word in the tinted box is *coal mining*.   (11 marks)

Test 40

40.1
1 lion
2 tiger
3 elephant
4 camel
5 leopard /ˈlepəd/
6 giraffe
7 zebra
8 monkey /ˈmʌnki/
9 bear /beə/
10 gorilla
11 goat
12 horse   (12 marks)

40.2
1 pets
2 wild; zoo
3 lamb
4 mice /maɪs/
5 insect
6 whales
7 chickens   (8 marks)

40.3

E	E	H	O	S	T	O	M	B	E
M	A	E	N	E	G	Y	U	R	
O	W	S	N	A	I	L	V	T	A
S	H	A	R	K	G	E	A	B	
Q	U	O	N	E	Y	L	W	E	B
U	N	B	E	T	F	L	E	R	I
I	S	P	I	D	E	R	E	F	T
T	R	E	E	D	O	B	L	N	
O	K	A	B	T	H	U	L	Y	S

(10 marks)

Test 41

41.1
1 France	5 Germany	9 Switzerland
2 Portugal	6 Italy	10 Greece
3 Britain	7 Holland	
4 Turkey	8 Spain	(10 marks)

41.2

Nationality	*Language*
Japanese	Japanese
Korean	Korean
Australian	English
Egyptian	Arabic
Brazilian	Portuguese
Argentinian	Spanish
Swedish	Swedish /'swiːdɪʃ/
Saudi (Arabian)	Arabic
Russian	Russian /rʌʃn/
Mexican	Spanish
Thai	Thai /taɪ/
Chinese	Mandarin / Cantonese (12 marks)

41.3
1 The Swiss	3 The Dutch	5 The Japanese	7 Germans
2 Americans	4 Italians	6 the French	8 Israelis (8 marks)

Test 42

42.1 forehead, eyebrows, cheeks, lips, chin, neck, shoulders /'ʃəʊldəz/,
chest, waist, hips, thighs /θaɪz/, knees, ankles (13 marks)

42.2 1 elbow   2 wrist   3 finger   4 nail   5 thumb (5 marks)

42.3 1 She's yawning /'jɔːnɪŋ/.   3 She's crying.   5 She's shaking her head.
2 He's smiling.   4 He's laughing. (5 marks)

42.4 1 bite /baɪt/   3 comb /kəʊm/   5 bend   7 breathe /briːð/
2 shake   4 fold   6 blow (7 marks)

Test 43

43.1 1 b   2 a   3 d   4 e   5 c (4 marks)

43.2 1 tall; slim/thin   4 strong/muscular /'mʌskjuːlə/
2 straight   5 good-looking/handsome   (6 marks:
3 dark   1 for each gap)

43.3
slim	skinny
plain	ugly
overweight	fat (6 marks)

43.4 1 a moustache /mʊ'staːʃ/   2 a beard /bɪəd/   3 a scar   4 a hairy chest (8 marks)

43.5 1 What does she look like?
2 How tall is she, exactly?
3 How much does she weigh? (6 marks)

Test 44

44.1 clever/bright; horrible/unpleasant; nervous/tense; easy-going/relaxed; pleasant/nice; stupid/thick (6 marks)

44.2
1 ambitious 3 cheerful 5 unreliable /ʌnrɪˈlaɪəbl/
2 unpleasant 4 inflexible 6 insensitive/inconsiderate (6 marks)

44.3
1 dishonest 3 unkind /ʌnˈkaɪnd/ 5 weak
2 mean 4 unfriendly 6 pessimistic (6 marks)

44.4
1 punctual 3 shy 5 initiative (12 marks:
2 sense 4 confident 6 miserable /ˈmɪzrəbl/ 2 for each)

Test 45

45.1
1 upset 3 frightened 5 jealous /ˈdʒeləs/
2 proud 4 embarrassed (5 marks)

45.2
1 happiness 4 jealousy 7 embarrassed
2 embarrassing 5 anger 8 embarrassment
3 pride /praɪd/ 6 sadness (8 marks)

45.3
1 whispered 3 march 5 stroll
2 shout /ʃaʊt/ 4 glanced 6 staring /ˈsteərɪŋ/ (6 marks)

45.4 1 e 2 c 3 f 4 a 5 b 6 d (6 marks)

45.5 1 of 2 on 3 at 4 of 5 at (5 marks)

Test 46

46.1
1 first 7 widower
2 full 8 single-parent / one-parent
3 middle 9 partner/girlfriend
4 surname /ˈsɜːneɪm/ / family name 10 close/old/good
5 only 11 step
6 inherited (11 marks)

46.2
1 uncles /ˈʌnklz/ 6 cousins /ˈkʌzənz/ 11 widow
2 aunts /aːnts/ 7 grandparents 12 step-father
3 brother-in-law 8 nieces /ˈniːsɪz/ 13 relatives/relations
4 sister-in-law 9 nephews /ˈnefjuːz/
5 mother-in-law 10 ex-wife (13 marks)

46.3 1 e 2 f 3 b 4 a 5 d 6 c (6 marks)

Test 47

47.1
1 born 5 split up / broke up 9 got
2 grew / was brought 6 went 10 had
3 met/saw 7 met 11 born
4 went out 8 fell 12 expecting (12 marks)

47.2
1 toddler 3 a teenager / an adolescent 5 early twenties 7 late forties
2 child 4 adult 6 mid thirties (10 marks)

47.3 1 childhood 3 rows /raʊz/ 5 retirement 7 marriage
  2 adolescence / your teens 4 middle age 6 old age 8 pregnant (8 marks)

Test 48

48.1 1 I live *on* my own. / I live *by* myself.
  2 I usually go *to bed* about midnight.
  3 Most nights I *get/go to sleep / fall asleep* very quickly.
  4 In the morning I have a shower and *(a) shave / get shaved*.
  5 I usually *have breakfast* about 7.30.
  6 After breakfast I clean *my* teeth.
  7 I arrive *at* work about 8.30.
  8 After work I sometimes *do* the shopping / go shopping. (8 marks)

48.2 1 fall 3 leave 5 late; wake up / get up 7 lie-in
  2 feed 4 break 6 stay in 8 play (9 marks)

48.3 1 oversleep 3 snack 5 washing-up
  2 nap 4 chat 6 cleaner (6 marks)

48.4 1 f 2 g 3 a 4 e 5 b 6 d 7 c (7 marks)

Test 49

49.1 1 garage 5 balcony 9 steps 13 terraced
  2 path 6 ground 10 doorbell
  3 fence 7 stairs 11 detached
  4 gate 8 roof 12 block (13 marks)

49.2 1 draughty /'drɑːfti/ 3 quiet
  2 tiny /'taɪni/ 4 enormous/huge /hjuːdz/ (4 marks)

49.3 1 This house belongs to a famous artist.
  2 The top room has a view of the forest.
  3 It's easy to heat the house.
  4 The house is in (a) terrible condition. (8 marks)

49.4 1 false (a semi-detached house is joined to one other house on one wall)
  2 true
  3 false (a landlord is the person you pay rent to)
  4 true: NB mortgage is pronounced /'mɔːgɪdʒ/
  5 true (5 marks)

Test 50

50.1 1 living/sitting; lounge /laʊndʒ/ 3 kitchen 5 spare /speə/ (6 marks:
  2 dining 4 bathroom 1 for each gap)

50.2 1 curtains /'kɜːtɪnz/ 4 TV remote control 7 coffee table
  2 armchair 5 lamp 8 vase
  3 carpet 6 **sofa** (8 marks)

50.3 1 **wash**ing machine 3 **dish**washer
  2 **cook**er/oven /'ʌvən/ 4 refrigerator/fridge (4 marks)

50.4 1 a food mixer 3 a saucepan 5 taps
  2 a kettle 4 a frying pan (5 marks)

50.5 1 d 2 e 3 g 4 a 5 c 6 b 7 f (7 marks)

Test 51

51.1
Bedroom	Bathroom
lamp	shower
pyjamas /pɪˈdʒɑːməz/	towels /ˈtaʊəlz/
wardrobe /ˈwɔːdrəʊb/	toilet
duvet /ˈduːveɪ/	bath
pillows	

(9 marks)

51.2
1 left/threw   3 went   5 mirror
2 switch/turn   4 set   6 have

(6 marks)

51.3
1 dirty; washing   4 did   7 get into
2 washing-up   5 put on   8 make
3 polish /ˈpɒlɪʃ/   6 housework

(9 marks)

51.4
1 chest of drawers /tʃest əv ˈdrɔːz/   3 alarm clock   5 **towel** rail
2 washbasin /ˈwɒʃbeɪsən/   4 bedside **table**   6 **house**work

(6 marks)

Test 52

52.1
1 working; **bat**teries   2 out (of) order   3 wrong with

(6 marks)

52.2
1 dropped; broke/smashed   2 spilt; stain/mark

(8 marks)

52.3
1 mood   4 ruined   7 tripped over   10 working
2 run out of   5 got   8 fell
3 burnt/burned   6 left   9 realised

(10 marks)

52.4
1 left   2 missed   3 got off   4 forgotten   5 lost   6 properly

(6 marks)

Test 53

53.1
(1) cheap (2) reasonable (3) quite expensive (4) very expensive
(5) incredibly expensive

(5 marks)

53.2
bought; spent; lent; sold; paid; cost (past tense and past participle forms
are the same for all these verbs)

(6 marks)

53.3
1 spent   4 afford /əˈfɔːd/   7 charged
2 lend; pay; borrow   5 saving   8 lend/give; borrowed
3 paid; cost   6 worth /wɜːθ/

(12 marks)

53.4
1 cost   3 currency; sterling   5 waste
2 standard   4 notes; coins

(7 marks)

Test 54

54.1
1 d   2 f   3 g   4 b   5 c   6 h   7 a   8 e

(8 marks)

54.2
1 He's got earache /ˈɪəreɪk/.   5 He's got a pain in his leg.
2 She's got backache /ˈbækeɪk/.   6 She's got a headache /ˈhedeɪk/.
3 He's got a pain in his arm.   7 She's got toothache /ˈtuːθeɪk/.
4 She's got (a) stomach-ache /ˈstʌməkeɪk/.

(7 marks)

54.3
1 sore /sɔː/   4 prescription   7 fillings
2 nose   5 hurt   8 injection
3 fever /ˈfiːvə/   6 painful   9 painless

(9 marks)

54.4
1 she's got flu (not 'a' flu)   4 His finger *was* injured /ˈɪndʒəd/
2 blowing *your* nose   5 a sore *throat* /θrəʊt/ *and a cough* /kɒf/
3 my back is very *painful*   6 hurt *myself*   (6 marks)

Test 55

55.1   1 sling   2 bruise   3 bandage   4 stitches   5 cut   (5 marks)

55.2   1 a   2 –   3 –   4 a   (4 marks)

55.3
1 collided *with* each other
2 one man *knocked* himself unconscious
3 cut *on* his forehead
4 an *ambulance* arrived
5 men *to* hospital
6 fifteen *stitches*
7 kept *in* hospital   (7marks)

55.4
1 fight /faɪt/; stabbed   4 swollen
2 shot   5 ankle
3 burnt; painful/sore   6 bleeding   (8 marks)

55.5   1 e   2 c   3 d   4 f   5 a   6 b   (6 marks)

Test 56

56.1
1 shirt   5 earrings   9 skirt   13 scarf
2 suit   6 necklace   10 tights   14 jumper/pullover
3 tie   7 blouse   11 boots   15 gloves
4 belt   8 jacket   12 hat   16 jeans   (16 marks)

56.2
1 I *took* off my clothes   4 too long
2 I got *dressed*   5 hung it *up*
3 it wasn't *big enough*   6 didn't *fit* me very well   (6 marks)

56.3
1 cuff   3 pocket   5 tights /taɪts/   7 size /saɪz/
2 collar /ˈkɒlə/   4 buttons   6 sleeves

1 down is *clothes*.   (8 marks)

Test 57

57.1
shop assistant; shop window;
window shopping; go shopping;
shopping list; shopping centre/mall (AmE); shopping basket   (6 marks)

57.2
1 clothes /kləʊðz/   3 stationery   5 electrical appliances/goods
2 toys   4 furniture /ˈfɜːnɪtʃə/   6 jewellery /ˈdʒuːlri/   (6 marks)

57.3
1 department store   5 boutique /buːˈtiːk/
2 **su**permarket   6 chemist('s) /ˈkemɪst/
3 butcher('s) /ˈbʊtʃə/   7 **news**agent('s)
4 **green**grocer('s)   8 shoe shop   (8 marks)

1 help   5 served   9 take
      2 looking for 6 try on   10 till / cash desk / counter
      3 size   7 changing room / fitting room
      4 looking   8 leave   (10 marks)

Test 58

58.1 1 cabbage /'kæbɪdʒ/   5 potatoes   9 grapes /greɪps/   13 apple
      2 peppers   6 green beans 10 melon   14 strawberries /'strɔːbəriz/
      3 carrots   7 peas   11 orange   15 peach
      4 cauliflower /'kɒlɪflaʊə/ 8 banana   12 pear   (15 marks)

58.2 1 mushrooms /'mʌʃruːmz/, aubergine /'əʊbəʒiːn/
      2 lettuce /'letɪs/
      3 cherries /'tʃeriz/; pineapple/pears /'peəz/
      4 oysters /'ɔɪstəz/; mussels /'mʌslz/
      5 veal   (8 marks)

58.3 1 false (lobster is a kind of shellfish)
      2 true
      3 true
      4 false (a calf is a young cow)
      5 false (salmon is a kind of fish)
      6 true
      7 false (aubergine is a different colour: it is purple) (7 marks)

Test 59

59.1 1 boil   2 fry   3 grill   4 roast   5 bake   (5 marks)

59.2 1 oven /'ʌvən/   6 put on
      2 courses; starter; main course   7 menu /'menjuː/
      3 heat   8 spic(e)y /'spaɪsi/
      4 service   9 sauce
      5 rare /reə/, medium-rare; well done 10 home-made   (14 marks)

59.3 1 tender   3 bitter   5 raw /rɔː/ / uncooked
      2 lean   4 tasty /'teɪsti/ 6 fresh   (6 marks)

59.4 1 a tip   2 book; in advance   3 an aperitif /əperɪ'tiːf/   4 bill   (5 marks)

Test 60

60.1 1 library /'laɪbrəri/   4 factory /'fæktri/
      2 car park   5 suburbs /'sʌbɜːbz/ / residential areas
      3 shopping centre   6 commercial centre/area   (6 marks)

60.2 1 noisy   3 stressful   5 peaceful   7 exciting
      2 polluted   4 crowded   6 safer   8 dangerous   (8 marks)

60.3 1 country(side)   3 wood   5 hedge   7 field
      2 valley   4 footpath 6 gate   8 tractor   (8 marks)

60.4 1 c   2 d   3 b   4 e   5 f   6 g   7 h   8 a (8 marks)

Test 61

61.1
1 traffic lights
2 **petrol** station
3 lorry
4 pavement
5 pedestrians
6 traffic jam
7 bend
8 road works
9 pedestrian crossing
10 junction
11 road sign
12 main road   (12 marks)

61.2
1 accident
2 rush /rʌʃ/
3 created/caused
4 overtake
5 into/onto
6 braked
7 prevent/avoid
8 direction
9 crashed/ran
10 injured /'ɪndʒəd/ /hurt /hɜːt/ /killed
11 damaged /'dæmɪdʒd/   (11 marks)

61.3
1 Go along this road
2 got in/into the car
3 Keep going
4 broke down
5 break the speed limit
6 overtook
7 turn left   (7 marks)

Test 62

62.1
1 lorry
2 coach
3 van
4 bus
5 bicycle/bike
6 motorbike   (6 marks)

62.2
1 run
2 fare /feə/
3 by
4 missed
5 platform
6 stop
7 arrival
8 due   (8 marks)

62.3

Train	*Plane*	*Taxi*	*Bicycle*
driver	pilot /'paɪlət/	driver	cyclist /'saɪklɪst/
drive	fly	drive	ride / cycle (without a noun)
get on	get on	get in(to)	get on(to)
get off	get off	get out of	get off
station	airport	taxi rank	(11 marks)

62.4
1 There was a long/big queue (of people waiting) for the bus.
2 The buses are always punctual.
3 Take this bus then change at Golden Square.
4 How much was your train fare?
5 The bus was full.   (5 marks)

Test 63

63.1
1 What do you do for a living?
2 How much do you earn? /ɜːn/
3 Do you have to pay income tax?
4 How much holiday do you get?
5 Do you have to work overtime in your job?
6 Do you get holiday pay?
7 Do you get sick pay?
8 What does your job involve?   (4 marks)

63.2 a 5   b 7   c 2   d 3   e 8   f 4   g 1   h 6   (4 marks)

63.3
1 attend
2 respon**si**ble for
3 running
4 do
5 seeing
6 responsi**bi**lities   (6 marks)

63.4 1 f   2 d   3 b   4 e   5 a   6 c   (6 marks)

63.5 1 I'm *a* builder and I work *for* a big company in the city of London.   (2 marks)
    2 Unfortunately, I haven't got a *job* at the moment, but I hope to find one soon.
    3 I work *in* a hospital in the X-ray department.
    4 What *does* your job *involve*, exactly?
    5 I have to deal *with* the delivery problems in my company.
    6 I *do* a lot of paperwork, which involves *filling* in a lot of forms.   (2 marks)
    7 I am *paid* a very good salary.
    8 I have to *advise* clients a lot in my job.   (10 marks)

Test 64

64.1 1 a lecturer /ˈlektʃərə/   5 a plumber /ˈplʌmə/
    2 an engineer /endʒɪnˈɪə/   6 a dentist
    3 a veterinary surgeon / vet /ˈvetɪnri ˈsɜːdʒən/   7 an accountant
    4 a carpenter/joiner   8 an electrician /ɪlekˈtrɪʃən/   (8 marks)

64.2 1 treat   3 look after   5 repair   7 design /dɪˈzaɪn/
    2 advise   4 operate   6 build   8 buy and sell   (8 marks)

64.3 1 a sailor in the navy /ˈneɪvi/
    2 a soldier in the army
    3 a policeman / police officer in the police force
    4 a firefighter in the fire brigade / fire service   (8 marks)

64.4 1 manual /ˈmænjuːəl/   3 medical   5 armed
    2 skilled   4 legal /ˈliːgəl/   6 emergency   (6 marks)

Test 65

65.1 1 Last week I went on a training course.
    2 The boss gave him the sack when he heard about the scandal.
    3 She resigned (from her job) because of the long hours.
    4 I am now responsible for both departments.
    5 His job involves a lot of travel / travelling a lot.
    6 I earned a lot / a high salary in my last job.   (12 marks)

65.2 1 same   3 same   5 different
    2 different   4 same   6 different   (6 marks)

65.3 1 I'd like to apply *for* that job, but I don't think I'll get it.
    2 He got a job *as* a manager in the shoe department.
    3 He's going *to retire* at the age of 60.
    4 We are giving him s*ome / a lot of* training to help him.
    5 He *was/got* promoted and they gave him a pay rise.
    6 I'm looking for a *part*-time job but I'll take anything which is interesting.   (6 marks)

65.4 1 earn   3 at   5 looking
    2 prospects   4 involves   6 resign /rɪˈzaɪn/   (6 marks)

Test 66

66.1 1 calendar   4 calculator   7 diary   10 files
    2 notice board 5 drawer   8 monitor   11 filing cabinet
    3 computer   6 wastepaper basket 9 keyboard 12 briefcase   (12 marks)

66.2
1 works
2 answers; arranges /əˈreɪndʒɪz/
3 send
    4 show
    5 does; filing /ˈfaɪlɪŋ/; writing   (4 marks: ½ for each gap)

66.3 1 c   2 e   3 b   4 f   5 d   6 a   (6 marks)

66.4
1 wrong: make/manu**fac**ture/produce
2 correct
3 wrong: check/e**xam**ine/inspect
4 correct
5 wrong: **pack**aged
6 correct
7 correct
8 wrong: delivered/sent/de**spatch**ed (*formal*)   (8 marks)

Test 67

67.1 A: 1 e   2 c   3 a   4 f   5 d   6 b   (6 marks)
B: 1 raw materials   2 tax cut   3 public expenditure   4 interest rate   (4 marks)

67.2
1 loan
2 bigger
3 **turn**over/revenue
4 well
5 inflation
6 recession
7 overheads
8 interest   (8 marks)

67.3
1 sharp
2 fall
3 interest
4 rates
5 falling
6 rise
7 slowly/steadily
8 rose
9 dramatically
10 make/manage
11 profit
12 loss(es)   (12 marks)

Test 68

68.1 1 product   2 price   3 promotion   4 place   (4 marks)

68.2
1 figures /ˈfɪɡəz/
2 research /rɪˈsɜːtʃ/
3 share /ˈʃeə/
4 forecast; target
5 leader   (6 marks)

68.3
1 compe**ti**tion
2 pro**duce**
3 representatives/reps
4 **mar**keting
5 competitor
6 **fash**ionable
7 distri**bu**tion
8 pro**mo**tion
9 con**sum**ers   (9 marks)

68.4
1 mass-produced
2 good value /ˈvæljuː/
3 reliable /rɪˈlaɪəbl/
4 **glam**orous
5 up-to-date
6 luxury /ˈlʌkʃəri/   (6 marks)

68.5
1 compete /kəmˈpiːt/
2 luxury
3 leaders
4 containers
5 department   (5 marks)

Test 69

69.1
1 collected stamps
2 play chess
3 go camping
4 play cards
5 play; instrument
6 collects; coins   (12 marks)

69.2
1 climbing /ˈklaɪmɪŋ/
2 jogging /ˈdʒɒɡɪŋ/
3 hiking /ˈhaɪkɪŋ/
4 spare /ˈspeə/
5 antiques /ænˈtiːks/
6 board /bɔːd/   (6 marks)

69.3
1 He is mad about DIY. / He is DIY mad.
2 I make all my own dresses.
3 We gave it up because it was just too expensive as a hobby.
4 She joined the tennis club last year.
5 I do a lot of camping in the mountains.
6 I took up photography when I was a teenager.   (12 marks)

Test 70

70.1
1 a (rugby) ball used in rugby /ˈrʌgbi/
2 a **crash** helmet used in **mot**or racing / motor cycling
3 (ski) sticks used in skiing
4 a (tennis) racket used in tennis
5 a (table tennis) bat used in table tennis
6 a (golf) club used in golf
7 **run**ning shoes used in athletics /æθˈletɪks/
8 (swimming) trunks /trʌŋks/ used in swimming

(12 marks:
1 for the equipment and
$\frac{1}{2}$ for the sport)

70.2
1 play; do   3 referee   5 umpire
2 crowd; stadium /ˈsteɪdiəm/   4 spectators/fans; pitch   (8 marks)

70.3   1 c   2 f   3 e   4 a   5 d   6 b   (6 marks)

70.4   1 threw /θruː/   2 kicked   3 passed   4 head/score   (4 marks)

Test 71

71.1
1 played/did   3 winners
2 nil; scored   4 score; result   (6 marks)

71.2
1 Spain lost 2–0 to Brazil / Spain lost to Brazil 2–0.
2 Holland won 3–2 against Denmark / Holland won their match against Denmark 3–2.
3 Peru drew 2–2 with Italy / Peru and Italy drew 2–2.
4 The latest score is 1–0 to England.   (8 marks)

71.3
1 booked; tackle   3 lap   5 **cham**pionship   7 served
2 league /liːg/   4 kick; **pen**alty   6 points   (9 marks)

71.4
1 the semi-final   5 a tie-break
2 a knock-out competition / tournament   6 sets
3 extra time   7 fifteen love
4 a penalty shoot-out   (7 marks)

Test 72

72.1
1 circle /sɜːkl/   4 stage
2 stalls   5 rows /rəʊ/ of seats
3 curtains /ˈkɜːtɪnz/   6 aisle /aɪl/   (6 marks)

72.2
1 cast; stars   5 play
2 director   6 reviews /rɪˈvjuːz/; critics/reviewers
3 subtitles /ˈsʌbtaɪtlz/; dubbed /dʌbd/   7 musical; performance
4 war /wɔː/   8 audience /ˈɔːdiəns/   (12 marks)

72.3   1 c   2 f   3 e   4 b   5 d   6 a   (6 marks)

72.4
1 a comedy   4 a science fiction /ˈsaɪəns ˈfɪkʃən/ film
2 a **west**ern / cowboy film   5 a thriller /ˈθrɪlə/
3 a **hor**ror film   6 an action film   (6 marks)

Test 73

73.1
1 composer   3 exhibition   5 sculptor /ˈskʌlptə/
2 classical   4 musical   (5 marks)

73.2 1 vio**lin**   3 piano /pɪ'ænəʊ/   5 cello /'tʃeleʊ/   7 drums /drʌmz/
       2 guitar /gɪ'taː/   4 flute   6 **sax**ophone   (7 marks)

73.3 1 composer   7 jazz
       2 novelist/author/writer   8 pop
       3 poet /'pəʊɪt/   9 solo artist
       4 dramatist/playwright /'pleɪraɪt/   10 **port**rait
       5 orchestra /'ɔːkɪstrə/   11 landscape
       6 conductor /kən'dʌktə/   12 abstract   (12 marks)

73.4 1 opera   3 short
       2 Gallery; artists/painters   4 writes/composes; performs/sings   (6 marks)

Test 74

74.1 1 daily   3 tabloids
       2 published/printed   4 broadsheets   (4 marks)

74.2 1 The magazine comes out every week.
       2 The paper has a circulation of 5 million.
       3 It says in one paper that they're getting married.
       4 They have no plans to marry, according to another paper.
       5 There isn't much foreign news in the paper.   (10 marks)

74.3 1 Train service (badly) hit by storms
       2 New row over job scheme
       3 Government to cut hospital waiting lists
       4 New talks begin next week
       5 Transport Minister to quit soon
       6 Banks back rescue package
       7 Employment is the key issue, says union
       8 New bid to go round world in hot air balloon   (8 marks)

74.4 1 headline   3 editor /'edɪtə/   5 forecast
       2 journalists /'dʒɜːnəlɪsts/; freelance   4 critic; review/write-up   6 **car**toon   (8 marks)

Test 75

75.1 1 licence /'laɪsəns/   2 **terr**estrial   3 dish   4 cable   (4 marks)

75.2 1 commercial   5 drama series
       2 comedy series /'sɪəriːz/   6 documentary
       3 **soap** opera   7 quiz /kwɪz/
       4 **current** a**ff**airs   8 chat   (8 marks)

75.3 1 What's on TV/television tonight?
       2 What time does the film start? / What time's the film on?
       3 How long does it last?
       4 Is the game live? / Is it live?   (8 marks)

75.4 1 to plug it in
       2 turn over
       3 turn the TV down
       4 turn the TV off
       5 switch it on   (10 marks)

Test 76

76.1 1 A: Hello.
B: *Is that* Susan?
A: Yes.
B: Oh hi. *It's* Maria. / *This is* Maria.
A: Hello, Maria. How are you?
B: *Fine* thank you. And you?

2 A: Hello?
B: Hello. *Is that* Mr Fantini?
A: Yes, *speaking*.
B: Oh good morning. *This is* / *My name is* Pierre Kaufmann.
I tried to phone earlier but the line was *engaged*.
A: Yes, I *made* a lot of calls this morning. (8 marks)

76.2
1 answerphone / answering machine	4 mobile /'məʊbaɪl/	7 reverse/transfer
2 fax	5 on	8 operator
3 get; box; cards	6 Enquiries /ɪŋ'kwaɪrɪz/	(10 marks)

76.3 1 the wrong number
2 she's out / she's not in; be back; leave a message; give her   (12 marks:
3 put you   2 for each gap)

Test 77

77.1
1 (VDU) monitor	3 printer	5 CD-ROMS	7 mouse
2 screen	4 keyboard	6 floppy disks	(7 marks)

77.2 1 b   2 e   3 a   4 c   5 d   (5 marks)

77.3
1 save	3 cut	5 print	7 memory
2 copy	4 paste /peɪst/	6 virus /'vaɪrəs/; crash	8 laptop	(9 marks)

77.4 1 false (many business people use *spreadsheets* /'spredʃiːts/ to arrange numbers and financial information)
2 true
3 false (people who are computer-literate find these machines *easy* to use)
4 true
5 false (*software* is the program you need to work the machine)
6 true
7 true
8 false (it's not easy)
9 true   (9 marks)

Test 78

78.1 3 nursery /'nɜːsəri/   5 primary /'praɪməri/   11 secondary; comprehensives
16 leave; get/find; stay (on) / continue / carry on   18 go   (8 marks)

78.2 1 false (you pay to go to a public /'pʌblɪk/ school; state schools are free)
2 true
3 false (PE is short for *physical* education)
4 false (it is usually divided into *three* terms)
5 true
6 false (the day's work is the daily *timetable*)   (6 marks)

78.3 1 go to university   4 politics   7 left school
          2 Economics is   5 to bed   8 at eighteen
          3 Physics /ˈfɪzɪks/   6 did you study/do   (8 marks)

78.4 1 Geography /dʒiˈɒɡrəfi/   4 Maths/Mathematics   7 Information technology
          2 History /ˈhɪstri/   5 French   8 Religious education
          3 Science /ˈsaɪəns/   6 Music   (8 marks)

Test 79

79.1 1 psychology /saɪˈkɒlədʒi/   6 engineering
          2 architecture /ˈɑːkɪtektʃə/   7 medicine /ˈmedsɪn/
          3 **politics**   8 agriculture /ˈæɡrɪkʌltʃə/
          4 philosophy /fɪˈlɒsəfi/   9 law /lɔː/
          5 chemistry /ˈkemɪstri/   10 sociology /səʊsiˈɒlədʒi/   (10 marks)

79.2 1 Bachelor /ˈbætʃələ/ of Arts   3 Master of Arts
          2 Bachelor of Science   4 Doctor of Philosophy   (4 marks)

79.3 1 go   4 passed   7 lasted   9 doing / carrying out
          2 did / got on 5 get   8 got   10 give
          3 took   6 do/study   (10 marks)

79.4 1 true
          2 false (a graduate is someone who has finished their first degree /dɪˈɡriː/)
          3 false (an MA is a degree that you get on a postgraduate degree course)
          4 true
          5 false (tuition /tjuːˈɪʃn/ is the teaching of your course)
          6 false (a postgraduate is a student doing a second degree course)   (6 marks)

Test 80

80.1 1 trial   3 **bar**rister; attorney /əˈtɜː(r)ni/   5 judge /dʒʌdʒ/
          2 accused; de**fen**dant   4 jury /ˈdʒʊəri/   (7 marks)

80.2 1 If you do something illegal /ɪˈliːɡl/
          2 they will question you
          3 you will be charged with the crime / they will charge you with the crime /kraɪm/
          4 it can be hard to prove /pruːv/ it in court
          5 they are not guilty /ˈɡɪlti/
          6 listen to all the evidence
          7 At the end of the trial /traɪl/   (7 marks)

80.3 1 The police said he (had) committed the crime.
          2 I don't think you have broken the law.
          3 I hope the police will investigate this case.
          4 The barrister couldn't prove he was guilty.
          5 In the trial, he was convicted of the crime.   (10 marks)

80.4 1 sentence   3 minor /ˈmaɪnə/; punishment; fine /faɪn/
          2 prisoner; cell /sel/   (6 marks)

Test 81

81.1 1 rape   3 burglary /'bɜːgləri/   5 murder /'mɜːdə/
      2 robbery   4 theft   6 shoplifting   (6 marks)

81.2 *Crime*   *Criminal*
      theft   thief
      robbery   robber
      murder   murderer
      rape   rapist
      shoplifting   shoplifter
      burglary   burglar   (6 marks)

81.3 1 illegal   4 install   7 self-defence
      2 stole   5 prevent   8 property
      3 safe   6 alone   9 allowed   (9 marks)

81.4 1 commits   4 money belt   7 manslaughter /'mænslɔːtə/
      2 broke into   5 yourself   8 speed
      3 on; lock/check/shut 6 punishment   9 at   (9 marks)

Test 82

82.1 1 monarchy /'mɒnəki/   3 democracy /dɪ'mɒkrəsi/; democrats /'deməkræts/
      2 republic; republicans   4 dictatorship; dictator /dɪk'teɪtə/   (7 marks)

82.2 In any order:
      socialism, liberalism, communism, fascism /'fæʃɪzm/   (4 marks)

82.3 1 beliefs   3 politician   5 democratic   7 governs
      2 elect   4 economic /ekə'nɒmɪk/   6 political /pə'lɪtɪkl/   (7 marks)

82.4 1 Prime /praɪm/   3 vote(s)   5 majority /mə'dʒɒriti/   7 election
      2 held   4 parliament   6 policy /'pɒlisi/   8 leader   (8 marks)

82.5 1 road   2 in   3 wing; on   (4 marks)

Test 83

83.1 1 identity card   5 exam certificate
      2 birth certificate /'bɜːθ sə'tɪfɪkət/   6 enrolment form
      3 driving licence /'draɪvɪŋ 'laɪsens/   7 landing card
      4 application form   8 TV licence   (8 marks)

83.2 1 application form   3 visa /'viːzə/   5 enrolment/registration form
      2 landing card   4 identity card   6 membership card   (6 marks)

83.3 1 expires /ɪk'spaɪəz/ / runs out; renew
      2 sign /saɪn/; signature /'sɪgnətʃə/   (4 marks)

83.4 1 When were you born? / What's your date of birth?
      2 Are you single or married?
      3 When did you arrive / get here?
      4 When are you leaving? / When do you leave?   (4 marks)

83.5 1 birth   2 status /'steɪtəs/   3 arrival   4 departure   (4 marks)

83.6 1 d   2 a   3 b   4 c

Test 84

84.1
1 conflict	4 invaded	7 attacking
2 territory /'terɪtri/	5 captured	8 defend
3 outbreak	6 retreated	(8 marks)

84.2
1 armies – correct; troop – incorrect: should be troops
2 air forces – incorrect: should be air force
3 correct
4 correct
5 aids – incorrect: should be aid; food supply – incorrect: should be food supplies (7 marks)

84.3
1 terrorists/guerrillas /gə'rɪləz/	5 war zone
2 hostages /'hɒstɪdʒɪz/	6 to release/free (a prisoner)
3 hijack/hijacking /'haɪdʒækɪŋ/	7 peace settlement / treaty
4 civilians /sɪ'vɪliənz/	8 to shell (8 marks)

84.4
1 released/freed	5 agree
2 run out of	6 fired /'faɪəd/
3 wounded /'wuːndɪd/ / injured /'ɪndʒəd/	7 bargain /'baːgɪn/ / negotiate
4 dead	(7 marks)

Test 85

85.1
1 environment	4 caused; global warming (2 marks)	
2 pollution	5 acid rain (2 marks)	(10 marks:
3 ozone layer (2 marks)	6 bank	1 for each gap)

85.2 In any order:
1 Try to save water.
2 Try to plant trees.
3 Try to recycle aluminium cans.
4 Don't throw away aluminium cans.
5 Don't waste water.
6 Don't cut down trees. (6 marks)

85.3
1 polluting	4 conservation	7 damaging
2 environmental	5 protection	8 industrial /ɪn'dʌstrɪəl/
3 harmful	6 destroying	(8 marks)

85.4
| 1 resources /rɪ'sɔːsɪz/ | 3 dumping | 5 waste |
| 2 rain forests | 4 fumes /fjuːmz/; factory /'fæktri/ | (6 marks) |

Test 86

86.1
1 taxi
2 boarding
3 luggage /'lʌgɪdʒ/ / baggage /'bægɪdʒ/
4 cabin crew /'kæbɪn kruː/ /stewards and stewardesses
5 hire /haɪə/ (5 marks)

86.2 1 f   2 h   3 e   4 b   5 a   6 c   7 d   8 g   (8 marks)

86.3 1 checked/examined; went   4 cruising/flying
2 takes; lands/arrives   5 pay
3 put; fasten /ˈfɑːsən/   6 weighed /weɪd/   (9 marks)

86.4 1 Which way is the baggage reclaim?
2 Where is the check-in (desk) for American Airlines?
3 Oh, dear, I think I left my camera in the departure lounge.
4 Did you have a good flight?   (8 marks)

Test 87

87.1 1 single room   3 twin room
2 double room   4 full board   (8 marks)

87.2 1 The room has its own bathroom.
2 Breakfast and dinner.
3 Expensive.
4 Bed and breakfast.   (4 marks)

87.3 1 bill   5 lift   9 reception
2 included   6 working; wrong   10 call
3 Excuse; get   7 order/get/call   11 tip
4 booked; season   8 booked/reserved   (14 marks)

87.4 1 receptionist   2 porter   3 chambermaid /ˈtʃeɪmbəmeɪd/   4 chef /ʃef/   (4 marks)

Test 88

88.1 1 have a good   4 spend a lot
2 do a lot   5 it (worth) going   (10 marks:
3 go out in   2 for each question)

88.2 1 cathedral /kəˈθiːdrəl/   4 fountain /ˈfaʊntɪn/   7 palace /ˈpælɪs/
2 castle /kɑːsl/   5 temple   8 art gallery
3 market   6 statue /ˈstætjuː/   (8 marks)

88.3 1 packed   3 souvenirs /suːvənˈɪəz/   5 lively   7 cosmopolitan
2 touristy   4 guidebook   6 historic monuments   (7 marks)

88.4 1 have/take   2 got   3 go   4 enjoyed   5 spending/staying   (5 marks)

Test 89

89.1 1 place   5 beach   9 **sun**block
2 rented   6 sand   10 **sun**burn/**sun**burnt
3 seaside   7 sunbathing /ˈsʌmbeɪðɪŋ/   11 **resort**
4 spending   8 **sun**tan lotion   12 various /ˈveərɪəs/   (12 marks)

89.2 1 We go for a stroll in the evenings. / In the evenings, we go for a stroll.
2 It is very difficult to get away at weekends. / At weekends, it is …
3 I prefer to put my feet up and do nothing. / I prefer to do nothing and …
4 I think they really enjoy the peace and quiet. / They really enjoy the peace and quiet,
I think.
5 We are going to have a picnic in the countryside.   (5 marks)

     a–3   b–5   c–4   d–2   e–1   (5 marks)

89.3   1 beach/sun umbrella   4 rough /rʌf/   7 rocks
            2 windy   5 waves   8 cliff
            3 tent   6 yacht /jɒt/   (8 marks)

Test 90

90.1   1 in   3 on   5 at/(US) on   7 in   9 on
            2 at   4 in   6 in   8 at   10 on   (10 marks)

90.2   1 incorrect. I'll wait *till/until* he arrives.
            2 correct
            3 incorrect. I have known her *for* a very long time.
            4 correct
            5 incorrect. We fixed the appointment *for* next Tuesday.
            6 incorrect. I'm seeing him *in* about a week's time.
            7 correct
            8 correct   (8 marks)

90.3   1 recently /'riːsəntli/   3 for ages /fər 'eɪdʒɪz/   5 the other day / recently
            2 a long time ago   4 for the time being   (5 marks)

90.4   1 seconds   3 decade   5 hours
            2 fortnight   4 century   6 minutes   (3 marks: $\frac{1}{2}$ for each)

90.5   1 takes   2 lasted   3 take   4 last   (4 marks)

Test 91

91.1   1 two hundred and twelve
            2 five thousand, three hundred and thirty
            3 three million, four hundred and fifty thousand
            4 four point five
            5 nought point seven five
            6 six point oh/nought /nɔːt/ five
            7 three and a half
            8 twelve and a quarter /'kwɔːtə/
            9 one and a third
            10 the fourteenth of March
            11 August the twenty-first
            12 nineteen ninety-eight
            13 nineteen hundred and ten / nineteen ten
            14 fifty-three per cent
            15 six oh three, three five seven nine
            16 minus ten degrees / ten degrees below zero /'zɪərəʊ/   (16 marks)

91.2   2 subtraction   3 multiplication   4 division   (3 marks)

91.3   *Sample answers (there are other possibilities)*
            1 Four and two is six. / Four plus two equals /'iːkwəlz/ six.
            2 Twelve minus four point five is/equals seven point five.
            3 Eight times four is thirty-two. / Eight multiplied by four equals thirty-two.
            4 One hundred and twenty-eight divided by two is/equals sixty-four.
            5 One hundred and twenty-eight times four / multiplied by four is/equals five hundred and
              twelve.
            6 Two hundred and forty divided by eighty is/equals three.   (6 marks)

Test your English Vocabulary in Use (pre-intermediate and intermediate)   **133**

91.4　1 odd; even /ˈiːvən/　　　　　　　　3 out of
　　　　2 majority /məˈdʒɒrɪti/; minority /maɪˈnɒrɪti/　　　　　(5 marks)

Test 92

92.1　1 far; long　　2 tall　　3 long; far　　4 high　　　　　(6 marks)

92.2
Adjective	Noun
long	length
wide /waɪd/	width /wɪtθ/ or /wɪdθ/
high/tall	height /haɪt/
deep	depth /depθ/

　　　　　　　　　　　　　　　　　　　　　　　　　　　　(4 marks)

92.3　1 The field is 50 metres long / has a length of 50 metres /ˈmiːtəz/.
　　　　2 The field is 20 metres wide / has a width of 20 metres.
　　　　3 The swimming pool has a length of ten metres / is ten metres long.
　　　　4 The swimming pool has a width of five metres / is five metres wide.
　　　　5 The swimming pool has a depth of two metres / is two metres deep.　(10 marks)

92.4　1 short　　　　3 narrow　　　5 thick
　　　　2 thin/slim　　4 long　　　　6 shallow　　　　　　　(6 marks)

92.5　1 corner　　2 couple　　3 rise　　4 size　　　　　(4 marks)

Test 93

93.1　1 a square /skweə/　　4 a semi-circle　　　7 a star
　　　　2 a circle /sɜːkl/　　　5 a triangle /ˈtraɪæŋgl/　8 an oval /əʊvl/
　　　　3 a rectangle　　　　6 a pyramid /ˈpɪrəmɪd/　　　　(8 marks)

93.2　1 grey /greɪ/　　2 turquoise /ˈtɜːkwɒɪz/　　3 pink　　4 purple /pɜːpl/　(4 marks)

93.3　1 a striped /ˈstraɪpt/ dress　　3 a floral skirt
　　　　2 a tartan /ˈtaːtən/ tie　　　4 a check(ed) shirt　　　(8 marks)

93.4　1 Yes　　　　　　　　　　　　　　6 Yes
　　　　2 No (90 degrees)　　　　　　　　7 Yes
　　　　3 Yes　　　　　　　　　　　　　　8 Yes
　　　　4 No (between light brown and yellow or white)　9 Yes
　　　　5 No (it's almost round but not necessarily small)　10 Yes　(10 marks)

Test 94

94.1　1 container　2 contents　　　　　　　　　　　　(2 marks)

94.2　1 a bag of shopping　　　　7 a tin/can of soup /suːp/
　　　　2 a bowl of sugar　　　　　8 a tube /tjuːb/ of toothpaste
　　　　3 a vase /vaːz/ of flowers　9 a box of chocolates /ˈtʃɒkləts/
　　　　4 a jug /dʒʌg/ of water　　10 a carton /ˈkaːtən/ of milk
　　　　5 a bottle of beer　　　　　11 a cup of coffee
　　　　6 a jar of coffee　　　　　　12 a can of cola　　　(12 marks)

94.3　1 piece/bit　　　5 pair　　　　　　9 pair
　　　　2 bit　　　　　6 bit　　　　　　10 bunch
　　　　3 sheet/piece/bit　7 slices /ˈslaɪsɪz/ /pieces
　　　　4 bunch /bʌntʃ/　8 slice/piece/bit　　　　　　(10 marks)

1 packet   3 herd   5 gangs/groups/crowds

        2 group/crowd   4 piece/bit   6 piece/bit   (6 marks)

Test 95

95.1   1 sounded   3 look   5 taste   7 sounded   9 looks

        2 feels   4 smell   6 smell   8 felt   10 taste   (10 marks)

95.2   1 looks unhappy/sad/miserable /'mɪzrəbl/

        2 sounds awful/terrible/horrible/loud

        3 feels soft/comfortable

        4 smells lovely/fantastic/gorgeous /'gɔːdʒəs/

        5 tastes strange/odd/funny/nasty/horrible   (5 marks)

95.3   1 hear   6 watch   11 touched

        2 see   7 listening   12 look at; see

        3 listen to   8 hold   13 heard; listening

        4 touch   9 see

        5 look at   10 pressed   (15 marks)

Test 96

96.1   1 No smoking   5 Out of order   9 Sold out

        2 Please do not disturb /dɪs'tɜːb/   6 No parking   10 Fragile /'frædʒaɪl/

        3 No vacancies /'veɪkənsɪz/   7 Nothing to declare

        4 Keep right   8 No exit   (10 marks)

96.2   Do not leave bags unattended

        No vacancies

        Please queue other side

        Silence examination in progress

        Mind /maɪnd/ your head

        Keep off the grass   (12 marks)

96.3   1 Please do not feed the animals/monkey

        2 Do not lean out of the window

        3 Mind the step

        4 Beware /bɪ'weə/ of pickpockets   (8 marks)

Test 97

97.1   1 **mem**ory/recollection   2 idea /aɪ'dɪə/   (2 marks)

97.2   1 stuff   3 thing   5 thing   7 stuff

        2 stuff   4 stuff   6 thing   (7 marks)

97.3   1 jacket / waistcoat /'weɪskəʊt/   6 dates/events/facts

        2 perfume /'pɜːfjuːm/ / after shave   7 ideas

        3 fact/point   8 bicycle /'baɪsɪkl/

        4 knife   9 events in my life

        5 medicine /'medsɪn/   (9 marks)

97.4   *Any three of these:*

        around, about, approximately /ə'prɒksɪmətli/, roughly /'rʌfli/   (3 marks)

A: What shall I do with this *thing*?

B: It's *a bit* dirty, isn't it?

A: Yes, (*a bit*).

B: Well, could you put it in the dishwasher? It's full, so you could put it on.

A: OK. What shall I use?

B: Oh, the *stuff* in the bottle under the sink. It's *sort of* green with a (*sort of*) red label.

A: Fine. And how long does it take?

B: *Roughly* an hour. And I just want to iron a few *things* as well.

(9 marks: 2 each for the correct insertion of *a bit*, *sort of* and *roughly*)

Test 98

98.1

British	American
lorry	truck
main **road**	**high**way /ˈhaɪweɪ/
biscuit /ˈbɪskɪt/	**cook**ie
lift	elevator
term	**semester*** (recently being used more in British English)
dustbin /ˈdʌsbɪn/	**trash**can
petrol	gas
flat	a**part**ment
film	movie
car park	**par**king lot

(10 marks)

98.2   1 sweets/candy   3 waistcoat/vest   5 tap/**fau**cet /ˈfɔːsɪt/
2 chips / **french** fries   4 **trou**sers/pants   (10 marks)

98.3   1 rubbish   6 crisps
2 holiday   7 vest
3 wardrobe /ˈwɔːdrəʊb/ /cupboard /ˈkʌbəd/   8 secondary school
4 **under**ground   9 autumn /ˈɔːtəm/
5 pavement /ˈpeɪvmənt/   10 return ticket   (10 marks)

Test 99

99.1   1 regret; tell/inform; unable
2 purchased /ˈpɜːtʃɪst/; premises /ˈpremɪsɪz/
3 require /rɪˈkwaɪə/; assistance   (7 marks)

99.2   1 guests /gests/   3 start again   5 so
2 start/begin   4 caught /kɔːt/   (5 marks)

99.3   1 marvellous   7 quite/very
2 cleverest / most intelligent   8 children
3 collect   9 convenient /kənˈviːnɪənt/
4 pounds   10 think
5 arrange   11 man/person
6 toilet   12 arrive   (12 marks)

99.4   1 Do you fancy going out?
2 We must get in touch with them soon.
3 I'm going to have a word with him.   (6 marks)

Test 100

100.1
1 United Kingdom
2 United Nations
3 British Broadcasting Corporation
4 Prime Minister
5 Member of Parliament
6 European Union
7 Valued Added Tax
8 as soon as possible   (8 marks)

100.2
1 OPEC /ˈəʊpek/	3 Ms /məz/	5 Dr
2 AIDS /eɪdz/	4 Saint or Street	6 personal computer

(6 marks)

100.3 1 so on 2 for example 3 in other   (6 marks)

100.4
1 veterinary surgeon /ˈvetɪnri ˈsɜːdʒən/ – vet
2 photograph /ˈfəʊtəgrɑːf/ – photo /ˈfəʊtəʊ/
3 advertisement /ədˈvɜːtɪsmənt/ – advert /ˈædvɜːt/ or 'ad' /æd/
4 influenza – flu
5 blackboard – board
6 refrigerator /rɪˈfrɪdʒəreɪtə/ – fridge /frɪdʒ/
7 bicycle /ˈbaɪsɪkl/ – bike /baɪk/
8 laboratory /ləˈbɒrətri/ – lab
9 sales representative – sales rep
10 aeroplane – plane   (10 marks)

Personal diary

Test	Word	Translation	Points to remember	Related words

Test your English Vocabulary in Use (pre-intermediate and intermediate)

Personal diary

Test	Word	Translation	Points to remember	Related words

Personal diary

Test	Word	Translation	Points to remember	Related words

Personal diary

Test	Word	Translation	Points to remember	Related words

Phonetic symbols

Vowel sounds

Symbol	Examples		
/iː/	sleep	me	
/i/	happy	recipe	
/ɪ/	pin	dinner	
/ʊ/	foot	could	pull
/uː/	do	shoe	through
/e/	red	head	said
/ə/	arrive	father	colour
/ɜː/	turn	bird	work
/ɔː/	sort	thought	walk
/æ/	cat	black	
/ʌ/	sun	enough	wonder
/ɒ/	got	watch	sock
/ɑː/	part	heart	laugh
/eɪ/	name	late	aim
/aɪ/	my	idea	time
/ɔɪ/	boy	noise	
/eə/	pair	where	bear
/ɪə/	hear	beer	
/əʊ/	go	home	show
/aʊ/	out	cow	
/ʊə/	pure	fewer	

Consonant sounds

Symbol	Examples		
/p/	put		
/b/	book		
/t/	take		
/d/	dog		
/k/	car	kick	
/g/	go	guarantee	
/tʃ/	catch	church	
/dʒ/	age	lounge	
/f/	for	cough	
/v/	love	vehicle	
/θ/	thick	path	
/ð/	this	mother	
/s/	since	rice	
/z/	zoo	houses	
/ʃ/	shop	sugar	machine
/ʒ/	pleasure	usual	vision
/h/	hear	hotel	
/m/	make		
/n/	name	now	
/ŋ/	bring		
/l/	look	while	
/r/	road		
/j/	young		
/w/	wear		